D1483346

# Margit

# Margit

## A Teenager's Journey
## through the Holocaust and Beyond

### MARGIT FELDMAN
### AND
### BERNARD WEINSTEIN

WITH A FOREWORD BY

## GOVERNOR JAMES E. MCGREEVEY

Distributed by
State of New Jersey
Commission on Holocaust Education

I dedicate this book to those who were close to me
and who perished in the Holocaust:

The Buchhalter Family
The Granat Family

and to my children's grandparents:

Theresa Granat Buchhalter
and Joseph Buchhalter,
who will always live in my heart and soul.

*Margit Feldman*

Margit's Journey

1. Home in Tolcsva, Hungary
2. Ghetto Satoraljaujhely
3. Auschwitz
4. Cracow
5. Auschwitz
6. Gruenberg
7. Bergen Belsen

Map of Margit's journey during the Holocaust. Numbers indicate the order in which she moved to each location.

# CONTENTS

# FOREWORD

As the clouds of collective amnesia hover over both Europe and America, arousing fear that the Holocaust and its lessons might be forgotten, Margit Feldman's chronicle of her experiences during the darkest days of human history are especially important. It is a chronicle of courage, endurance, and faith.

The pain and devastation of the Holocaust are so profoundly searing as to defy articulation. However, the historical and ethical imperative to remember and to bear witness requires that we speak, even if the words uttered are halting and painfully inadequate. To be silent would be to doom the six million killed in the Holocaust to utter eradication, for now, though dead, they live on in our memory, pure and innocent, especially the one and a half million children who were murdered. Part of what distinguishes human from brute is the capacity for recording history and for retrospection, and therefore to forget would diminish our own humanity.

I first met Margit through the Council for Holocaust Education, to which she and I were both appointed by Governor Kean in 1984. I was immediately struck by Margit's capacity, despite the horror of having survived four death camps, to see the goodness and decency in every individual. I count her among my closest friends. Her story is one of great pain and incredible loss, but also one of great dignity and hope.

The lesson of the Holocaust is that when confronted with absolute evil, we cannot respond equivocally, with a sort of diplomatic etiquette that seeks ephemeral safety at the expense of freedom and decency. We must be ever vigilant. We cannot afford to be complacent about iniquity or the suppression of human rights anywhere, for the forces that prompt some to commit genocide are still alive.

Margit Feldman is not only a survivor; she is a gifted speaker and an extraordinary human being. As you read this book, let her words—and also the images they create and the lessons they teach—touch your heart as they have touched mine. You will agree that the world is blessed to have a woman of Margit's strength and character. Her life story teaches us never to despair of mankind. We pray for a world in which the weak will be secure and the strong compassionate—a world redeemed from the dark abyss of the Shoah.

James E. McGreevey
Governor
State of New Jersey

# ACKNOWLEDGMENTS

Many people inspired and contributed generously to the account of my journeys:

My husband, Harvey, who has given me his constant love, concern, and support. I could not have persevered in writing this book without his encouragement.

My children, Tina and Joseph, whose names immortalize the memory of my beloved mother and father, who perished in the *Shoah*; my dear grandchildren, Caryn, Joshua, and Zachary, who represent for me the continuity of my family; and my daughter-in-law Julie.

The many friends, teachers, students, and others who not only constituted an audience to my story, but provided encouragement, compassion, and affection that continues to inspire my educational mission.

I thank Marlie Wasserman of Rutgers University Press for her guidance and wisdom in getting this book into print.

My heartfelt appreciation and thanks go to my very dear friend and co-writer Dr. Bernard Weinstein, who worked with me for two years to make this journey a reality. Without his guidance, help, and encouragement, this would not have been possible. Bernard, Todah Rabbah.

Margit Feldman

# PROLOGUE

One of the earliest and most vivid memories I have from the little Hungarian town in which I spent my childhood is of a summer evening when I climbed a ladder to the outside attic of our house and watched a nighttime religious procession to a nearby cemetery. In this attic we used to store hay for the cows and horses so that they would have food for the winter. I recall sitting on the top step of the ladder, inhaling the pungent odor of the hay, and looking down into the valley. On this starry night I could see clearly across the valley above which our property was slightly elevated.

I looked across at the cemetery emblazoned with lights, a sight that communicated to me both eeriness and great beauty. As I sat there, I imagined the other side of the ocean. I knew I had aunts and uncles and cousins in a distant place called America. My favorite childhood reading had always consisted of geography books about faraway places, and I constantly wondered about that place called New York, teeming with people, noise, and gigantic structures that touched the clouds. I mused about the fact that, while it was night where I was, it was day there, and I wondered what the family members I had never met were doing at that very moment. Were they eating breakfast?

Going to school? Working? Little did I realize at the time that one day I would be living there!

Since that summer evening, so deeply embedded in my memory, I have made many journeys, including the one that brought me to America. For better or worse, my journeys have given a shape and a purpose to my life.

Margit Feldman

# INTRODUCTION

"You shall not stand by idly while your neighbor bleeds."
*Leviticus* 19:16

In 1945, a Hungarian-Jewish girl named Margit Buchhalter, just past her sixteenth birthday, lay in a hospital bed in Carlstad, Sweden. She was afflicted with pleurisy and diphtheria, and she was still suffering the effects of wounds caused by an explosion that had taken place in Bergen-Belsen, from which she had recently been liberated. Within the previous year she had experienced the horror of four concentration camps and a death march. She had lost nearly seventy members of her family on the day they arrived in Auschwitz. Two of the three remaining members of that family had died only scant weeks before in Bergen-Belsen.

In the hospital Margit experienced, for the first time in more than a year, human affection, tender gestures, kindly smiles, and soft voices. The language was unfamiliar, but the meaning behind the words and gestures instantly communicated itself to her. After the barbarous cruelty and callous indifference of the concentration camps, she found empathy and sympathy among ordinary Swedish people whom she had not even known and who had not known her, yet had comforted and aided her in the hospital and would continue to do so upon her release. She later described them as her "guardian angels."

In time Margit began to realize, however, that the gestures and voices she encountered in the hospital, and the aid and encouragement she received over the subsequent months, were conditions of her helplessness. She realized also that she would ultimately have to leave the hospital, and perhaps the country, without having been able to establish any living connection to her past. At that point, connecting with the American side of her family was a faraway dream. She had not yet fastened on the idea of immigrating to Palestine. For weeks after she experienced these realizations, she lived suspended between the memories of recent horrors and a future that seemed a yawning abyss. Her only surviving relative, her Uncle Henrik, had gone back to Hungary, the place to which she had sworn to herself never to return.

Much later, Margit would break that vow—once, in 1972, to visit her surviving uncle, and again, in 1996, to lay claim to possible reparations for the losses her family had endured at the time of their deportation. But in that earlier period in Sweden, her return to her home was unthinkable to her. She thought nothing could ever be as it had been.

As her body and spirit were slowly healing in the hospital, she had the time and leisure to reflect. In that interval the seedbed of an idea was lain that would not fully take root until years later. She was haunted by the fact that, while the Jews of Hungary were being deported and murdered, the outside world had done nothing to end their agony. She remembered that her gentile neighbors, people she had known all of her early life, had stood idly by for the most part, observing the decimation of Jewish life in her town. She remembered, too, that even the Allies, who were probably aware, by mid-1944, of what was happening to the Jews in the death camps, had nevertheless failed to intercede in their behalf.

Eventually the seeds planted in the Carlstad hospital during those early postwar days flowered into activity as pain, loss, and blighted memory slowly became transfigured into a process whereby Margit would share her remembrance with the public for the enlightenment—and warning—of future generations. After living many years in America, she found a challenge, a mission, and a release in telling her story to others. Her message is that the *Shoah* is not merely a Jewish issue, but a human issue, and that one must be neither a collaborator nor a bystander in the face of evil.

Whenever Margit Buchhalter Feldman tells her story to audiences, she offers this reflection: "On April 16, 1944, my world went up in flames and the free world remained deathly silent." Her personal narrative has acquired a very special resonance, reaching multitudes of persons each year, most significantly the young. She has consistently, bravely, and resolutely broken through the deathly silence of the past in order to bear witness, to inform, and to educate others about the crimes of the *Shoah* and the sins of apathy and ignorance. Her story is that not only of a survivor of and witness to atrocity, but also of a messenger to present and future generations.

In New Jersey, where she has made her home for almost fifty years, Margit Feldman has dedicated much of her life and energy to the cause of Holocaust education. Through telling and retelling her story and through the process of helping to make her community and state active centers of learning about the Holocaust, she has reached hundreds of educators and thousands of students. She has helped to enhance the cause to which she has given much of her life.

One of the harshest lessons Margit learned as she, her parents, and her grandmother were being evicted from their home in Tolcsva, Hungary, was that driven home by her neighbors' indifference. She describes how their belongings, "which [they] were never to see again, were placed upon wagons owned and driven away not by strangers, but by neighbors and long-time friends." Among those was a man whom her father had known for decades, had befriended, and had served with in the First World War. She recalls also from that terrible day how neighbors ran into the vacated Jewish homes, seizing whatever property they could appropriate, while still others watched, impassively or coldly, the pitiful procession of Jews being herded to the schoolyard, where they had been ordered by the Hungarian gendarmes to assemble. But, as she was soon to realize, these portents were only a prelude to the horrors of the ghetto, of Auschwitz, of Cracow, of Gruenberg, and, finally, of Bergen-Belsen.

Unlike other European nations, in which the murder and deportation of Jews had begun, at the very least, a year earlier, Hungary had retained its Jewish population until the spring of 1944, when the Nazis finally occupied it. Hungary had seen Hitler's early victories and the war itself as an opportunity to expand its territory into Czechoslovakia, Yugoslavia, and Rumania. Alliance with Germany made that possible. Germany saw Hungary as a hedge against the Soviet Union, and therefore as an ally and partner. Indeed, in June 1941 Hungary entered the war against the Soviets on Germany's side. Although the whole process of "cleansing" Hungary of Jews was delayed, the inevitable Nazi takeover of the country finally did occur, even as the tide of war was turning and Germany was already verging on defeat.

Hungarian Jews fell into two main groups. One group was aware of what was taking place elsewhere in the Nazi-dominated world; the other, at a distance from centers of communication, had only a fragmentary sense of what was going on outside their regions. The first group either was in a state of bewilderment as to when the axe would fall upon them or clung to the vain hope that the imminent defeat of Germany would prevent the axe from falling altogether. The second group was unable even to *imagine* the axe itself. The Buchhalter family belonged to the second group.

Margit's father was one of those who could not conceive of his country's aiding and abetting the destruction of its Jews, despite the evidence of both attitudinal and legalized Hungarian anti-Semitism. After all, he reasoned, he had fought for the Austro-Hungarian Empire in the Great War of 1914–1917, as so many other patriotic Jews had done. Furthermore, living in a small, rural agricultural community like Tolcsva made it unlikely that a family of modest means would have much access to the outside world. The Buchhalters did not even own a radio. The newspapers sold in Margit's father's store carried no news of Jewish annihilation, nor did local radio broadcasts announce what was happening to Jews in other parts of Europe.

Of course, Margit's family was not oblivious to Hungarian anti-Semitism or unconscious of extreme nationalism. They knew well enough that Jews were easy and accessible targets of defamation and violence. Why, after all, did Margit's concerned father regularly follow her at a discreet distance as she walked each day to the Jewish school she had to attend? Weren't Jewish children frequently beaten and verbally tormented for their "odd" appearance by their gentile peers? While attending school briefly in Budapest, had Margit herself not experienced a sense of isolation even in her academic success because others saw it as a mark of her "Jewishness"? Even as a very young child, had she not felt more spontaneous pleasure playing with her farm animals than with the gentile children, most of whom, she felt, wanted only access to the toys she owned? Didn't religious anti-Semitism reveal itself, particularly during the Easter season?

However, it was her father's incarceration, along with that of other Jewish men, in a forced labor camp in 1943 that had provided Margit and her family with a convincing omen of a sinister future. Still, the abrupt dislocation of her father from the family nucleus, the suddenness of the Nazi occupation, and the removal of Margit and her family from a familiar world to the alien and hellish existence of the ghetto seemed an inexplicable nightmare.

The shock that Margit and her family experienced was probably replicated in the lives of thousands of other Hungarian Jews, who until March 1944 had lived in relative "safety." From the outbreak of the Second World War until the Nazi occupation, Hungary's political leadership had alternated between two distinct sets of individuals. One set had tried to distance themselves from Hitler and from the task of isolating and deporting the Hungarian Jews (Pal Teleki, 1939–41, and Miklos Kallay, 1943–44). The other set had consisted of puppets of Nazi Germany (Laszlo Bardossy, 1941–42, and Dome Stojay, 1944, who replaced Kallay and presided over the deportations, which began in the Carpathian region where Margit lived). The fate of the Jews alternated according to the degree of commitment of each Hungarian prime minister to following the demands of the Third Reich.

Very likely, no group of Jewish nationals within the Nazi-occupied world suffered more the cruel dilemma presented by the need to interpret mixed signals than did the Hungarian Jews. The imposition of the laws defining and excluding Jews, implemented in the late 1930s by Prime Minister Béla Imredy, had slowed down somewhat under Teleki and intensified under Bardossy, only to be resisted by Kallay, the first prime minister to be strongly advised by Nazi Germany to deport Hungarian Jews. Finally came the Nazi occupation of March 19, 1944. The fate of Hungarian Jewry was sealed.

Margit's father, like many Hungarian Jews, was a small entrepreneur. He ran a general store and a modest farm on which the family lived and raised livestock. Despite Imredy's early regulations, Joseph Buchhalter's previous war service would have exempted him from adherence to harsh quotas imposed on Jewish professionals and business people by the process of "Aryanization." Though wholesale Aryanization did not take place until the Nazi occupation, severe restrictions were imposed by the middle of 1942, and Margit's father's general store suffered economic decline when he was arbitrarily forbidden to deal in certain merchandise and or to carry on specific business functions.

While the Buchhalters' economic means began to diminish noticeably, they could still afford the necessities of life and had the means to celebrate holidays and gather together with their extended family. Family and faith were still central to their lives and provided comfort amid uncertainty and growing dread.

At the time of her father's incarceration and her mother's assumption of both parents' responsibilities, Margit herself underwent an initiation into adulthood. Her childhood precocity and idealism faded into a mature acceptance of limiting circumstances and a sober sense of responsibility. While her mother took her father's role in running what was left of his business, Margit took over many of the domestic chores.

Her father's return signified the last period during which her family would be together. The reunion took place shortly before the German occupation, which, unwelcome as it was to most Hungarians, seemed to them a lesser evil than Soviet domination. When the Kallay forces began secret negotiations with the Western Allies, the Nazis, aware of what was taking place, foresaw disaster in rapprochement between Hungary and Germany's enemies. The occupation commenced, therefore, with Kallay ousted and Stojay, the Nazi puppet, installed.

The extreme right-wing, nationalistic Hungarian groups, including the Arrow Cross, began to initiate their own "Final Solution" just before the conclusion of Passover 1944, when the rounding up of Hungarian Jewry began in the first of six "zones": Carpatho-Ruthenia. Here lived the Buchhalters and most of their extended family. During the dark month in which they were imprisoned in the ghetto, situated in Satoraljeujhely, the county seat, they never saw a German soldier or S.S. officer. Those who enforced the brutal laws of the ghetto were their own countrymen. Margit saw her first German S.S. officer while boarding the train that was to carry her and her family to Auschwitz.

Soon after her arrival in Auschwitz came Margit's separation from all that she had known: first the irretrievable loss of her loving and protective parents, then a momentary and accidental encounter with a fellow prisoner and distant relative that doubtless saved her life. She then clung desperately to her Aunt Elizabeth and Sarika, Elizabeth's sister-in-law, with whom she survived the selection for death. After two months in Auschwitz, she, Elizabeth, and Sarika were shipped to Cracow. But then they were returned to Auschwitz, and in the course of camp life Margit underwent a change. She describes her return from Cracow to Auschwitz for her second stay there:

> I was only four months older than the healthy and active young girl who had been driven into the ghetto with her family, but I was like an automaton. I followed orders and did what the S.S. told me to do every day. I no longer worried about the consequences of things. But I was already wiser, less innocent. I knew exactly what the smoke meant, what the chimneys were for. I knew that the Germans were burning human flesh, that people were being turned into ashes. The

odor of burning flesh was unmistakable and unbearable. It entered us through our nostrils and burned our eyes. I knew that the people who were being turned into charcoal were transports, as I had been in what seemed like centuries ago. Now the realization of what had happened to my parents, my grandmothers, my aunts and uncles, and my younger cousins assaulted me vividly.

Perhaps the turning point had come even earlier in Cracow when Margit had witnessed fellow prisoners randomly shot and realized fully the fragility of her own existence. "Will I still be alive at the end of the day?" she asked herself constantly. As she was living through the waking nightmare of the camps and the death march that took her and other prisoners to Bergen-Belsen, all her attention was focused on her moment-to-moment survival, on overcoming near-death experiences, on pain, starvation, disease, wounds, and the sorrows of loneliness and abandonment.

Once rescued from the hell of her confinement in Bergen-Belsen, once she realized that she was utterly alone in the world, and once physically healed in the Swedish hospital, Margit began to think of going to Palestine. It was then that the American side of her family made the chance discovery that she was searching for them. A path was created. At the end of it was life in America: a childhood fantasy fulfilled. All Margit's attention would now be centered on beginning a new life.

In America she found, miraculously, many loving and welcoming branches of both parents' family trees. Her aunt, Minnie Boehm, her father's sister, who was to die in 2000 at the age of 103, became a devoted surrogate mother, and hosts of other relatives materialized, bringing her joy, comfort, and friendship that helped see her through the continuing illnesses and hospitalizations engendered by her physical suffering in captivity.

Margit's marriage to Harvey Feldman, a young New Yorker whom she met while convalescing in a hospital, provided her with a family of her own. They moved to New Jersey, raised two children, worked together to build a business, and made friendships that exist to this day. Margit possessed all the external attributes necessary to create a shield of forgetfulness to protect her from a tragic past.

Nevertheless, she was drawn back into that past in the early 1970s, when her children, Tina and Joseph, were in different stages of adolescence. She was driven by the desire to see her Uncle Henrik, who had remained in Hungary, yet she was petrified by the memories her return might evoke. The journey she finally embarked upon reawakened harsh and bittersweet memories. Later in the same decade she reluctantly acceded to a request from a friend's son that she tell the story of her Holocaust experiences to his high school class. Although Margit feared at first to stand before a group, she made an audiotape, the impact of which on those who heard it was so strong that she finally determined to speak in person to students and teachers. She realized a role for herself as a living and breathing witness to the horror she had experienced, a witness with whom young people might identify. She would recreate for them the fourteen-year-old girl standing between life and annihilation. In her talks she points out, "This is not a fiction. This is my life, and it is still a part of me."

In recent years Margit's mission has been to deny the deniers and revisionists of Holocaust history, as well as the skinheads, Hitler devotees, and neo-Nazis who are able to reach secondary school and college students and others through the Internet, militia groups, and even "scholarly" journals.

One of her most important achievements was the creation of an annual spring program at Raritan Valley Community College in North Branch, New Jersey, which three thousand students attend each year to obtain information and participate in workshops on the Holocaust and other episodes of genocide. Margit also spearheaded the drive to create the Holocaust and Genocide Resource Center at Raritan Valley. She served for several years on the New Jersey State Commission on Holocaust Education and was one of those instrumental in making Holocaust and genocide education mandatory in New Jersey.

Beyond what Margit has done in Holocaust education, she has served the Jewish community by working tirelessly for the Central New Jersey Jewish Home for the Aged and was a past president of the Jewish Federation of Somerset, Hunterdon, and Warren Counties. She has dedicated herself particularly to helping the vulnerable and the powerless. She fulfills the Jewish mandate of loving one's neighbor as oneself, and above all, she affirms by her deeds her unwillingness to be a bystander.

I first met Margit Feldman twelve years ago, when I interviewed her for the Oral Testimonies Project on the Holocaust at Kean College in Union, New Jersey, where I teach. Since then, she has spoken to my classes and seminars on countless occasions and has become a dear friend. I have had many opportunities to hear her tell her story to young people of high school and middle school grades, and the effect she has on these students and their teachers is virtually indescribable. Somehow the narrative always seems as fresh, natural, and deeply affecting to me as to first-time listeners.

Margit Feldman and I have written this story in such a way as to reflect Margit's voice over a period of years, a voice that bears witness to one of the greatest evils of the twentieth century yet remains rational, humane, and aware of the human capacity for both goodness and evil. In telling the story of her early years and the Holocaust period, we have endeavored as much as possible to capture the voice of the young girl, sheltered by a calm and loving world, who was forced to encounter the maelstrom of loss, violence, and cruelty. In writing about the American period, we have tried to reflect both the voice of a maturing woman adjusting to a new environment, new branches of her family tree, love, marriage, and children and the voice of the settled citizen bringing compassion and enlightenment to her community, and particularly serving the young.

In addition to the narrative itself we are including testimonies and letters from family members, as well as photographs. The testimonies and letters give voice to the people closest to Margit—her husband, children, and oldest grandchild—in order to enable them to express what she has meant to them.

Bernard Weinstein

# 1

# *Childhood*

---

I was born to an Orthodox Jewish family on June 12, 1929. Much later I learned that I came into the world on the very same day as another infant whose name would one day be known throughout the world: Anne Frank. Sixteen years later I was rescued from Bergen-Belsen, one of the most infamous of all the Nazi concentration camps. Anne Frank, who had also been in Belsen when I was there, had not been so lucky, however. She had died in that very camp shortly before it was liberated. When I speak to groups of students and teachers, I carry two large photos, each of a young girl still in childhood: one is of Anne Frank; the other is of me. I feel that there is an inextricable bond between us, since it might so easily have been I, not she, who perished in that infamous place.

My parents' names were Joseph Buchhalter and Theresa Granat Buchhalter. The place where I grew from infancy to my teen years was Tolcsva, in northeastern Hungary near the Czechoslovak border.* That region was known as Zemplen Megye, of which the county seat was Satoraljaujhely, one of the most populous Hungarian-Jewish enclaves outside of

*For this and other locations associated with Margit's early life, see the map on the reverse of this book's dedication page.

Transylvania. However, I was actually born in Budapest. Because my mother was unable to deliver me on her own, the Tolcsva doctor advised my father to take her to the Polyclinic, the largest hospital in Budapest, and it was there that I first came into the world. I was actually one of a pair of twins, but my brother died in childbirth.

Perhaps because of the circumstances of my birth, one of my earliest ambitions was to study medicine and become a doctor in Tolcsva. My goal as a young girl was to help to improve medical facilities there, so that the lives of babies about to be born would not be put at risk and so that no pregnant woman, ready to deliver her infant, would have to go somewhere else to give birth.

Although medicine in our town was far from advanced, I found a role model in our family doctor. His name was Klein, and he was a kindly man with a soft voice and a gentle touch who visited our home whenever one of us was ill. He was a bachelor, and he dedicated himself to his patients, who consisted of virtually everyone in and around Tolcsva. At the age of eight I contracted scarlet fever. I remember how Dr. Klein came to our house each day to examine me. I had been isolated in a separate room with my grandmother, who volunteered to care for me. I was burning with fever, I recall, but she was at my side whenever she could free herself from her chores. At first I was certain I would never leave my bed again. But when Dr. Klein first came into my room, he immediately applied cold compresses and made me take some bitter-tasting medicine. But all the while he would assure me, "Muncika, you will be well soon, and be able to run around and play." I never forgot the warmth in his soft voice.

Tolcsva was a small agricultural community, with a population of two thousand to twenty-five hundred people, of whom approximately one-tenth were Jews. Though it was only a *shtetl* (village) in size, Tolcsva was well known and was visited by hundreds of outsiders. It was situated in a region of Hungary, around the city of Tokaj, that was known for its vineyards. Even today, it is a mecca for wine connoisseurs. The main street had all the stores, and this was where the farmers brought their goods three times weekly to display and sell.

Tolscva had a small restaurant with rooms in the back for travelers. The hotel's proprietors, a family named Prince, were Jewish, but there was no restriction on their clientele. Many non-Jews stayed there, too. The dietary laws of Judaism were strictly observed, however. There was also a theater in the center of town where plays were staged. Outside our town, and in the direction of the mountains, there was a popular spa where people, often from other towns and cities, went for health and recreation. I can remember horse-drawn carriages going past my house carrying vacationers to the spa. It was commonplace to hear singing and shouting as the vacationers passed by.

We were a fairly prosperous community, thanks partly to Tolcsva's vineyards and the popularity of the spa. But on the outskirts of town lived laborers and gypsies, and most of them, particularly the gypsies, knew discrimination and poverty. The gypsies were always regarded as social outcasts. In general, the rest of the community avoided them. The only contact we had with them was during a festival or parade. They would participate in the festivities and perform for the rest of us, and people would throw coins at them. I recall them driving through Tolcsva in their multicolored, decorated wagons. The music they played was very melodic, often lively, but sometimes melancholy. I often wished I could just get up on the makeshift stage and join them in their dancing. I wondered, though, how they could dance and play their violins, given the sad condition of their daily lives.

My father ran a general store. His merchandise consisted mostly of food supplies. His customers were both farmers and laborers. The laborers would often spend their salaries on wine and would then charge their purchases. Yet my father's patience and kindness were boundless. He had sympathy for everyone. When some of his customers drank up their wages, he altruistically "forgot" to enter into his ledger the money owed to him, and simply gave to the mens' families the supplies necessary to sustain them until the next pay period. This postponement of payment might continue for a long time, and it sometimes provoked heated discussions between my father and my mother. His argument always went something like this, "Theresa, it's not his children's fault that he drinks up his week's wages! Do you want them to starve?" The logic of this was irrefutable, but the dilemma persisted: how long could payments be delayed without our suffering, too?

Usually on Mondays, Wednesdays, and Fridays we had what is called today a "farmers' market," to which people brought the produce they hoped to sell. I remember seeing live chickens, ducks, and geese waddling about the market. I would follow my mother around and watch her as she bargained with the various vendors. Virtually everyone was, at least in part, a farmer.

There was also a thriving lumber business within our town in which my father's family was for many years engaged. They sold lumber for furniture and for firewood so that houses could be heated in winter. For a time my father worked in the lumber business, before he took over the general store. His younger brother Sany, however, continued in the business, supplying lumber to furniture factories.

My father had another brother named Henrik who lived with his wife and two daughters, Edith and Erzsike, in Sarospatak, a neighboring town northeast of Tolcsva. Henrik was in charge of the Jewish community in Sarospatak. In Sarospatak lived also my Grandmother Buchhalter. My father's sister, Elizabeth, lived with her husband in Satoraljaujhely, which later became the Jewish ghetto for the area in which we lived. They owned a restaurant and published a local newspaper. I remember boys on bicycles riding through town and delivering the papers. My Aunt Elizabeth had an elegantly furnished five-room apartment on the town's main thoroughfare. I loved to visit her there.

Since she had no children of her own, Aunt Elizabeth took pleasure in spoiling me. She would take me shopping for clothes and prepare my favorite foods. She was always beautifully groomed and wore the most stylish clothes with flair. Her makeup was always perfectly applied. She was dark complexioned, with luminous brown eyes. She had curly hair arranged in the style of the movie stars of the time.

My mother's two brothers, Danesh and Jeno, lived in Budapest with their families. Uncle Danesh, who had beautiful red hair and bore a tremendous resemblance to my grandfather, was a furniture maker. Uncle Jeno, who was dark haired and had the same huge, sunken eyes as my grandmother, was an accountant. My mother's older sister, Hermine, and her husband lived in a smaller town between Budapest and Tolcsva. They owned a butcher shop. How I used to look forward to their visits and all the joyous times we shared! We saw them all at least twice a year.

We were a fairly prosperous community, thanks to Tolcsva's vineyards, its lumber business, and the popularity of the spa. But on the outskirts of town lived laborers and gypsies, and most of them, particularly the gypsies, knew discrimination and poverty. The gypsies were always regarded as social outcasts. In general, the rest of the community avoided them. The only contact we had with them was during a festival or parade. They would participate in the festivities and perform for the rest of us, and people would throw coins at them. I recall them driving through Tolcsva in their multicolored, decorated wagons. The music they played was very melodic, often lively but sometimes melancholy. I often wished I could just get up on the makeshift stage and join them in their dancing. I wondered, though, how they could dance and play the violin, given the sad condition of their daily lives.

Tolcsva never had a shortage of water. The town is situated close to the Tisza River. In the middle of our street was a well that pumped water for the area, although we were fortunate enough to have our own well. Behind our house was a brook that bubbled with fresh water, so the fishing was very good there. Here I spent many summer days with my father. While he fished, I swam. In between large, moist stones could be found enormous shrimps and lobsters that our gentile neighbors used to pull out. As a very young child I was afraid to go near the rocks because I was sure the live lobsters would bite me. But when the summer heat came, I could not wait to run to the brook to cool off.

Yet water was frequently a danger to our region as well. One of the dreaded seasonal occurrences came during the spring thaw, which brought torrential rains, mud, and, worst of all, flooding. There were no drainage facilities, so we were constantly inundated with water. Sometimes the water came up to our very house. Often furniture and household items were ruined by water seeping into the house.

Even worse for us was the destruction of merchandise in our general store. This proved terribly costly to my parents. Cleaning up afterward was an immensely difficult task. I remember spending whole days mopping up and trying to retrieve items that hadn't been ruined in the flooding. The whole Tolcsva community suffered from these floods, even the animals. At these times we were in harm's way both economically and physically.

My childhood, as I remember it, was happy and secure. As an only child I was the center of my family's attention. My parents doted upon me. We also shared our house with my maternal grandparents, who provided me with an additional loving influence, although my grandfather died in 1935, when I was only six. In our house lived a young woman who did domestic chores for us. A laundress came in once every two weeks.

I can recall as a very young girl standing by my mother's side and watching as she readied her dough for baking or scrubbed the pots or swept the floors. I carry with me also a strong mental image of my maternal grandmother daily calling to and feeding our chickens, geese, ducks, and turkeys. She would take me by my small hand as a child, saying, "Come, Muncika," and leading me to the chicken coops where we collected eggs each day. She made a game of it, and I looked forward to it each time. I can recall how, when the chores were done, I would often sit with my mother and grandmother in the parlor and listen to their reminiscences about their early lives and the difficulties and deprivations with which they had lived when they were younger. "We want you to have the comforts and security we never had," my mother would tell me.

Since we inhabited an agricultural area, we had a small farm. We raised quite a few animals on our farm. As a young child I regarded the cows, chickens, ducks, geese, and turkeys as my "playmates." I remember playing with them for hours on end. I loved to imitate the sounds they made. When I did something wrong and wanted to hide from my parents, I would lie down in the barn inside a clump of hay, and I would feel that the cows and calves were watching over me, protecting me from my parents' punishment. I cannot ever forget how emotionally attached I was to the animals among which I grew up.

We kept pigeons so tame they would fly down to accept breadcrumbs from my hand. My father once constructed a ledge just above our living room windows for the pigeons nesting there. I sat at the window for hours, just watching them fly back and forth. I envied them. "How nice it would be," I said to myself, "just to be able to fly anywhere I chose to, and then come back!" The most pleasurable part of the experience was to watch the mother pigeon lay an egg and to wait until the baby was hatched. I always had the opportunity of feeding the infant pigeons, even during nesting season. They were so tame they would fly down and accept bread crumbs right from my hand.

Each of the seasons of my childhood produced vivid memories for me. I loved springtime, when nature came alive. My mother kept a flower garden. Each spring, she and I would plant flowers that bloomed through the summer. She had certain perennial bushes that she would take indoors in the winter and bring out again in the spring. These bushes had the brightest pink, white, and yellow flowers I have ever seen. In the middle of the courtyard was a magnificent lilac bush that I can still see vividly in my mind's eye. I have tried to duplicate this bush in my own yard, but without the success my mother had.

Today my daughter, Tina, plants flowers every spring for me to enjoy. By this simple act she brings back new memories of my mother, whose namesake she is. Tina will never fully know what her action means to me. It is in her that my mother still lives for me.

We also had a good-sized garden where we grew our own vegetables. The mixture of fertilizer and cow manure provided us with a less-than-pleasant aroma, but it made our soil rich and gave us the freshest vegetables I've eaten to this day. As I grew older, during springtime I was able to help my father bring the cows and calves to pasture.

During the summer months, my friend Katy Klein, who lived in Satoraljaujhely during the rest of the year, came to Tolcsva to stay with her grandparents. During those times we were constant playmates and companions, sharing meals and activities. We developed a friendship that is ongoing even to this day. Katy, whose married name is Roth, now resides in Cleveland, Ohio.

Another girlhood friend with whom I am still in contact is Cilike Friedman (née Green), whose father was the baker of Tolscva. She now lives in Los Angeles.

When my mother cooked chicken soup during the summer, I would go to our garden and pick fresh parsley, kolrabe, carrots, celery, and dill. The joy of doing all these things made them seem to me less like chores than play. They were also to be preparations for my own adult life.

We and our next-door neighbors, the Fishmans, also Jewish, planted fruit trees on which grew delicious *szelva* (white and purple plums), *barac* (peaches), and *cheresznye* (white and red cherries), which I can still taste. During the summer months, little tomboy that I was, I loved to climb these trees and pick the fruit, which I would eat while sitting atop a branch. Sometimes I stayed up in a tree so long that my mother would have to come looking for me. In my remembrance I can still taste the delicious fruits and vegetables I had then, and I associate them with the delightful summers of my childhood.

During autumn there was little time for leisure activities, as we were involved in harvesting wheat and corn. The annual corn harvesting was always a joyous occasion for us. We would go to one another's homes to husk the corn and to get it ready for drying. Some of the kernels were roasted so that we could taste the sweetness of the corn we grew. Once it was dried, we removed the kernels from the corn. While a portion of the kernels was used to feed the poultry, the rest was ground into cornmeal for our own consumption.

One event I can sharply recall to this day was the annual autumn harvesting of the grapes for wine making. For my family and the whole region, the grape harvest was a vital aspect of our economic well-being. Yet the harvest was also a time of holiday. We drove to the vineyards from miles around in horse-drawn carts. I used to run around the fields tasting all the grapes—green, purple, and dark ones. The laborers would cut grapes off the vines and put them in baskets that they carried on their backs. Once the baskets were full, they would empty them into the barrels on the wagons. To make the wine the people would first wash their feet and then stamp on the grapes to get all the juice out. Later the wine would be taken to cellars for aging. We would have a day toward the end of the harvest when we made jams and jellies, which we stored in jars for the winter.

At harvest time, my Aunt Elisabeth would bring us sardines and fresh bread at lunchtime in the field. Our lunch concluded with *babka* and other pastries that my mother had baked, and also iced coffee. I can recollect the gentile workers cooking bacon and pork nearby. The pungent aroma of the meat drove us insane because it was so tempting, and yet pork was prohibited for us as Jews. However delicious our own food, we yearned for " forbidden fruit."

In the winters I loved to go on excursions with my father in a horse-drawn sleigh amid the snow–covered mountains of northern Hungary. It was one of the few opportunities I had during the year to have my beloved father to myself. As the horse and sleigh transported us through the winter scenery, which reminded me of pictures in a child's storybook, he would tell me stories of the history of the region, entertain me with songs, and describe the winters of his own youth with his brothers and sisters amid the majestic mountains. Now and then we saw a deer or an elk run by. We even saw red foxes. Before we left on these excursions, my mother would provide us with plenty of warm blankets to shield us from the blinding cold, and when we returned home we would find that she had already prepared hot cocoa and home-baked cookies for us.

As I remember these early years, our lives seem to me to have been deeply attuned to the rhythms of nature and to the presence and unity of family and community. I feel even now that I had little reason to fear the future.

CHAPTER

2

# Faith and Aspirations

As a child I always looked forward to the Jewish holidays. Because we were Orthodox, our extended family, which was spread around the whole region in which we lived, was forbidden to travel in order to be together for the high holy days and the major festivals. Yet I will remember forever the wonderful smells of cooking and baking in preparation for these special times of the year.

Most precious to me was the weekly Shabbat (Sabbath), which Jews celebrate from sundown Friday till sundown Saturday. I would awaken early every Friday morning in order to work by my mother's side at Sabbath preparations. She wanted to prepare me to do my own household chores when I grew up. On Friday afternoons when I returned from school, I would experience the intoxicating odors of chicken soup and roasting poultry and noodle pudding, as well as challah and *babka* baking in the oven, in preparation for our Sabbath meal.

On Friday nights (and on Sabbath mornings) I would accompany my father to the synagogue. I would carry his prayer shawl in its little sack. Once we returned home after service on Friday evening my father would conduct a beautiful kiddush (the blessing said over the wine and the challah), and I would say the prayer with him. My mother, father, grandmother, and I would then sit down to our Sabbath meal.

My mother never knew how many people would be at our Sabbath (or holiday) table. My father often brought to our table yeshiva students far from home and strangers from other towns to share in our hospitality. He believed in the literal application of the Biblical admonition to welcome the stranger in our midst. He would say to the strangers he met at our synagogue who might be from another town, "No, you're not going to walk back. Just come back with me, and take a seat at our table." My mother would always have more than enough prepared for all of us. Even today, I cannot cook merely for the immediate members of my family; I invariably remember that anyone might unexpectedly come by. This was part of my parents' heritage to me.

There were always two sets of Sabbath candlesticks, one for my grandmother and one for my mother. These were made of sterling silver and were polished vigorously for each holiday. Late in the evening as we readied for bed, our gentile neighbor, whose name was Huszak, came to extinguish the lights. (Jewish law forbids Jews to light fires, turn lights on or off, or perform any other kind of work on the Sabbath.) On a recent visit to Hungary I met Mrs. Huszak again. She reminded me that she had been our "Shabbat goy" (a gentile hired to perform the tasks that Jews are forbidden to do on the Sabbath).

Our synagogue was located on the main street of Tolscva. On Sabbath mornings when I was very young, I divided my time in the synagogue between the downstairs, where my father and the other men prayed, and the upstairs, where the women sat. When I sat with my mother, she would open her "goodies bag" and give me pastry or *babka* to munch on. Once

I reached my early teens, however, I had to sit upstairs and pray "seriously" alongside my mother and my grandmother.

Our rabbi's name was Kornitzer. His nephew, Bela, who immigrated to the United States, became a famous historian and an advisor to Presidents Roosevelt and Eisenhower. I revered Rabbi Kornitzer, and I even had a "crush" on his son during my early adolescence. His daughters were dear friends of mine. In the last tragic days of the Holocaust, I witnessed the deaths of his wife and youngest daughter in Bergen-Belsen.

Years later, while living in Bound Brook, New Jersey, I went with the Ladies Auxiliary of the Bound Brook Hospital on a fund-raising excursion to Plainfield, where a cosmetologist had a salon. Her name was Alicia Karpati. Once we arrived and she made some introductory remarks, I began looking around and saw diplomas from Budapest and heard her discussing matters with her husband in Hungarian. I asked Alicia when they had arrived in America and where they were from in Hungary. I told them I was from Tolcsva.

At this point she turned white, approached me, took my arm, and immediately saw the numbers tattooed on them. She then led me upstairs to her living quarters, where she revealed that she was the niece of Rabbi Kornitzer of Tolcsva! She asked me to tell her if I knew what had happened to the members of her family. I told her I had been with her aunt and her two cousins in Bergen-Belsen and had seen her aunt and her younger cousin die of diphtheria and starvation. We were both overcome with emotion and tears. Once she composed herself, we went down and told the rest of the group what we had discovered. Shortly after that we left, but Alicia and I developed a warm friendship that lasted until she left the area and moved to Florida. After that we lost contact with each other.

I remember Rabbi Kornitzer as a sagacious teacher, a compassionate rabbi, and a commanding presence in the synagogue. His family always welcomed me into their home.

Once I was older, following service I was dispatched to pick up a traditional Sabbath dish: *cholent,* a casserole made of beans, meat, and potatoes that was cooked overnight in a baker's oven. We were not allowed to cook at home on Friday night or Saturday. I would bring the *cholent* home, where we would eat it as the Sabbath midday meal. This dish was so delicious that just the smell was enough to arouse my appetite.

On Saturday night after the *havdalah* service, which separated the Sabbath from the rest of the week, my mother would take a fish my father had caught in the brook during the week, which she had prepared on Friday, and served it cold under a layer of dill. I still recall the exquisite taste—a recipe I have been unable to recreate in my own home. Nothing tastes the same as it did in Hungary!

Everything we needed for religious purposes was accessible to us. Tolcsva had a kosher butcher who served as a *shochet* (kosher slaughterer) and whose shop was located on the grounds of our synagogue. We lived in a community that was largely open and heterogeneous. Jewish families in Tolcsva were not concentrated in one sequestered, segregated area, as in a ghetto, but were spread around the entire town.

My father was so religious that when I took sick with scarlet fever and had to be quarantined with my grandmother in our guest bedroom, he would put on his prayer shawl and phylacteries and pray all day. When my fever ran very high, he made a pilgrimage to the famous Liskai Rabbi, considered by Orthodox Jews to be a miracle worker. From that town my father returned to Tolcsva with some earth from Palestine wrapped in a cloth. The cloth was tied around my neck, and my father felt in the deepest recesses of his heart that this was what finally broke my fever and made me well.

I recall that when I was somewhat older my mother became very sick and was taken to Satoraljaujely to the hospital. I understand now that she was suffering from a very bad case of phlebitis, an inflammation of the veins in her right leg, and the doctor in Tolcsva could not cure her. In the hospital, the doctors wanted to operate on her leg, but my father again went to the Liskai Rabbi, who came to see my mother and told her to follow his orders—specifically, to cut off her beautiful hair and to begin wearing a *shetl* (the wig that Orthodox married women wore to show their reverence for God). The rabbi told her that this would make her well; he also promised to pray for her. To be sure, she did get better without surgery. That is how deeply my parents believed in their religion, in the rabbi, and in God.

In Tolcsva we also had a *cheder* (a Hebrew school) where the boys were studying the *Torah*, *Mishna*, and *Gemara* and all of the other interpretations and commentaries pertaining to Jewish law. In the schoolyard lived the shammes (sexton) of the synagogue. He was also one of our religious teachers. He had a wife and six children, some of whom were close to me in age and were my playmates.

Being an only child, I didn't feel the pressure of competing with siblings for my parents' attention and admiration. My only-child status made me somewhat demanding. I was a very fussy eater, and I often rejected the food my mother prepared. Perhaps this was the result of not having to compete with siblings for portions. My mother would insist on my tasting everything, whether I liked it or not; however, my grandmother would go stealthily to the chicken coop and fetch eggs, which I loved, and prepare them for me in ways that I liked. Thus she kept me from "going hungry," something I would learn the meaning of all too soon.

Being an only child also made it easier for me to succeed in school, and thus to please my elders. School was a magnet for me. I looked forward each day to getting up and going there. In addition to geography, I excelled in mathematics. Spelling, however, was my nemesis.

My interest in school did not prevent me from exercising simple vanities. I desired beautiful clothes. When my father traveled to shop for his store, he would always bring back materials for a blouse or a skirt for me. I would then run to a dressmaker whom my mother used, and she would help me make the clothes from the materials that my father had purchased. We had a primitive sewing machine at home that we operated by foot, and the process of using it was always a joy to me. My mother also used to send me regularly to the home of a lady who taught me how to knit, embroider, and crochet.

During the time I was growing up, schools in the region were parochial, although they were supported by the government. The largest school was Catholic. However, Jewish children, who numbered somewhere around sixty, attended a Jewish day school. Most of the neighborhood children were, of course, Christian. Although there was always a degree of distance and tension between Christians and Jews, we generally got along tolerably. But I recollect more fondly the joy I felt playing in the schoolyard and outside the synagogue with my Jewish friends. I did have a number of Christian playmates as well, though I am certain that part of the reason we associated with one another was that I had an abundance of toys, sent to me by my family in America, with which they loved to play.

Even as a young child I was conscious of a prejudice against Jews. Very religious children, dressed in traditional clothes, were frequently tormented by gentile children both verbally and physically. Most Jewish children and parents accepted it as a natural condition of being Jewish in a non-Jewish world. But I recall that when I went to school as a child, my father followed me at a discreet distance in order to make certain no harm came to me. I pretended not to notice that he was doing this. Neither one of us would acknowledge his reason, even later on, but I knew that his act was a sign of concern for me.

Education in Tolcsva was limited. Students of promise found little benefit in staying there. Even though I was their only child, my parents realized this. When I was about eleven they made arrangements to send me to Budapest to live with Danesh, my uncle, who was a skilled and relatively prosperous carpenter and furniture maker. I attended school in Budapest for one year. It was the farthest I had ever traveled until that time. That was in 1941, and the situation for Hungarian Jews was perceived to be worsening to such a degree that my father eventually became convinced that I would be safer returning to live at home in Tolscva.

Had my maternal grandfather been alive at the time, I should probably never have been allowed to go to live with Danesh and his family, since he had intermarried with a gentile woman and they had a son who was raised as a non-Jew. Because of this, my grandfather observed the required seven days of mourning, known as *shiva,* for his son. He sat on the customary pine box, wept, and lamented. He regarded Danesh as dead. This was considered customary among Orthodox Jews whose children married non-Jews.

On his deathbed, my grandfather was urged even by my grandmother to forgive and make peace with his son. Indeed, Danesh himself came to Tolcsva to plead for his father's forgiveness. I will never forget seeing him standing outside my grandfather's window crying, looking into the house, and pleading for any sign of acknowledgement and pardon.

Yet my grandfather was unable to bring himself to forgive his son, and I am certain that he died filled with agonizingly conflicting emotions that both tortured him and yet made it impossible for him to relent. His family pleaded with him: "You cannot die in peace because you're not forgiving your son." But so imbedded in him was his Judaism that he resisted. My grandmother, however, did forgive her son. Ironically, Danesh was to die under Nazi rule as a Jew. I was never able to learn what happened to his wife and only son. When I went to Budapest in 1972, I tried to look up his family, but I could not find them or any record of them.

The school I attended in Budapest was a secular one. I remember that I had to wear a uniform there, and, in general, no one stood out in a crowd. Still, I was continually pointed out as "the Jewish girl." If one were Jewish, one didn't forget one's "difference." I worked hard to get good grades. This was not always easy, because the competition was keener and the teaching methods and the school system were far more rigorous than what I had known in Tolcsva.

Because I was diligent and got good grades, I was given a grudging acceptance by my peers. Often gentiles attributed academic success to the "Jewish brain" or to what they perceived as the competitive Jewish drive for acceptance. It made me unhappy to hear these opinions. I was being labeled; however, I knew that my diligence and academic success came not from being Jewish, but from the great sacrifices my parents had made to send me to Budapest. I knew my absence was a hardship to them, so I worked extra hard to justify it. When I was home they had counted on me to help with chores; now they were shorthanded, and life would be more difficult, particularly for my mother.

In Budapest, despite the tensions there seemed to be much more mingling between Jews and non-Jews than in Tolcsva.

There was little overt animosity; rather there was a subtle sense of "otherness" that was cloaked in outward civility.

While I was in the large city I got used to a very different life from what I had known in Tolczva. I was reminded of the fable of the country mouse that visited his cousin in the city. At home I reveled in the bucolic atmosphere, serene and predictable and familiar. The large city, however, throbbed with variety and excitement and color. All around me were theater, opera, and cafés, as well as finely dressed people—all the luxuries of modernity, and all of these appealing to the sensibilities of a naive adolescent.

My Uncle Danesh lived in a beautiful house with indoor plumbing and hot and cold running water. The young Jews I met in Budapest lived lives far more sophisticated and luxurious than the ones I knew from home.

Life in Budapest was not altogether pleasurable for me despite its "glamor." When I was invited to the homes of school friends, I would silently compare the modern luxuries they enjoyed with what now seemed the rural and backward character of my home in Tolcsva. I felt a pang when I considered how many more "refinements" of life they were accustomed to than I was. Furthermore, while living at my uncle's house I was required to do household chores, such as drawing the water for my uncle's bath. I was not catered to as I had been at home, and I must admit that I resented the state of "servitude" in which I suddenly found myself. At home the chores had seemed a form of play at being an adult; here they assumed the more serious nature of obligation.

If Budapest was different from Tolcsva, the Tolscva that I returned to seemed far different from the one I had left. Once I was sent home because of the increased sense of danger in Budapest, Tolcsva appeared to me even more rustic and I experienced a sudden void. Having tasted the big city, I felt I had "grown up" and was eager to spread my wings beyond the rustic limitations of my early years.

Life for all the Jews in our area was also becoming more ominous. Anti-Jewish discrimination had increased noticeably and had been codified into laws. During my absence, my parents had had to give up our domestic servants. They had been forced even to dismiss the woman who had done our laundry every other week. My mother became a domestic herself, cleaning, milking the cows, and doing all the chores she had previously been spared. Once I returned home, I had to help her so that she could assist my father in running what remained of our business. I did numerous chores: I learned how to milk a cow, how to knead the dough for bread and challah and cakes, and how to clean the house. The privileged life of childhood had suddenly been torn away from me. I could feel my life changing perceptibly. The "city mouse" was forced, once again, to become the "country mouse," and the transition was not easy.

Thus I entered my teenage years.

CHAPTER

3

# Ominous Signs

I knew little of what was going on in the rest of Europe. Probably the same could have been said of many Hungarian Jews. But I would often hear my parents whisper to each other in Yiddish, which they assumed I didn't understand, although I knew certain phrases from having heard them repeated. One such phrase that my father used was "*Is vert nisht gut zein*" (It's not going to be good). Once in a while, he would make some oblique remark or other to me about "black clouds overhead" that would sooner or later "burst." Yet he never specified what he meant. Quite honestly, I can't truly estimate what my father or my mother knew or didn't know, as they never discussed these issues with me.

I overheard my parents say, and I also heard from others, that Hungarian-Jewish merchants would no longer be allowed to sell certain products: sugar, coffee, flour, various oils—all items that my father sold in his general store. My father could no longer sell products that required coupons. Jews were now forbidden to take their wheat to be processed into flour. I remembered how in the past my father had taken the wheat he grew to the nearby town of Liszka. Now he had nowhere to take it. As a result of all these prohibitions, our income diminished drastically.

As I was an only child, my parents watched over me, dutifully shielding me from any sign that boded peril or disruption. My early life had centered on family, friends, holidays, school, animals, and flowers. I had known little of the harsh realities of anti-Semitism or of the plight of Jews in other parts of Europe, whose economic security and physical safety were being threatened and whose very lives were being annihilated.

My father, whose strength and love had sheltered me, could hardly believe what was happening. After all, this was the country in which he had lived, of which he had been a faithful citizen, and for which he had fought bravely in the Great War of 1914–18, suffering wounds and becoming a decorated officer. (I have pictures of him in his uniform. I even have pictures of him wounded, with nurses taking care of him. An aunt who came to America before I did brought them over with her, and later she gave them to me.) How could his compatriots now look upon him as an outsider? I don't know what my father would have done had he realized what we would ultimately face. But under the circumstances, as a soldier, patriot, and loyal citizen of the former Austro-Hungarian Empire, he refused to believe the worst.

People in Budapest, no doubt, were more aware of the international scene and of what had befallen the Jews of Poland, the Soviet Union, Western Europe, and other parts of Central and Eastern Europe than were people in rural areas like ours. I now know that at least the prominent Jews of Budapest had access to information. But for those of us who lived in the rural parts of Hungary, the last country whose Jews were to be deported, there was no coverage of what was happening to our people. There were no radios in Tolczva. Even though my father sold newspapers in his store, there had been no real news to inform us of what was taking place, and virtually nothing filtered in from outside—or it was simply ignored by the press.

There was no opportunity to verify the rumors that spread around our community. My father was therefore adamantly committed to remaining in the land of his birth. Although his sisters, who had moved to America much earlier, had begged him for years to take his family out of Hungary and bring them to America, and although my mother's brothers were willing to send papers, his reply was invariably, "This is my country. I served it, I protected it. It would never do me any harm." It was a plaintive and futile attempt at self-reassurance, spoken as though the nation of Hungary was an entity apart from its population!

Certainly I, like most of my Jewish contemporaries, had always known that there were some lines we could not cross. Being Jewish set us apart from everyone else. We could not, for example, mingle too closely with our non–Jewish neighbors during their Christian holy days, when the priests and other clergy thundered forth from their pulpits such epithets as "Christ–killer" and roused their congregants against Jewish "perfidy." We knew to maintain our distance during these times.

Often I tried to answer other children's charges of "You killed Christ" by saying, "Do I look like a killer? Do my mother and father look like killers?" But one could not reason against the hateful accusations spawned from the misinformation given to them from early childhood at home and at church.

My family was helpless in other ways as well. We knew, for example, that some neighborhood children raided our coops and stole chickens and also committed other forms of vandalism. On many nights after we put out the lights and went to sleep, we were awakened by strange noises and barking dogs. I would hear one of my parents say, "There is someone on our property!" But we would stay in the house, waiting until morning to assess the theft or damage. Often raids went on all through the night. Eventually we even took the dogs inside, since we found one of them dead one morning. By that time, things were becoming more ominous.

But we hardly felt real danger so long as we remained within the bounds of discretion. What we feared most was malicious retribution in the form of theft and vandalism of property. We knew we could not accuse the children of stealing without incurring the wrath of the whole gentile community. The possibility of encountering hostility from our non-Jewish neighbors, whether religiously generated or not, kept us even more rooted within our own community.

Yet there were handfuls of local people who appeared to know more of the situation we were in and who could assess it better than we could. A gentile family named Kovacs, who lived across the way from us, had a son who had been a military officer and was now in the Hungarian diplomatic service. This young man spoke to my father and, having been trained as a diplomat both literally and figuratively, used rather vague words like "taken" and "resettled," strongly implying that something deadly was being prepared for the Jews. Exactly what did the word *resettled* mean? We ourselves had never thought of a concentration camp. We thought, "We're probably going to be taken from our homes and put to work someplace, perhaps even in another country." At the time, this seemed terrible enough!

But my father shrugged off the young man's words, arguing that nothing like that could occur in the country of his birth. It is extremely difficult for me to evaluate my father's thoughts and actions at that time. Do I blame him for not taking these warnings to heart? I'm not certain what alternative he had. Had he permitted himself to imagine what would actually happen, he might have committed some desperate act, short of taking his life or killing his family as sometimes happened among people marked for a terrible fate.

I myself while playing with the Kovacs children, overheard the talk of the adults. I must admit that I hardly conceived, from the bits and pieces of information I had, that they were speaking about us or that what the adults were discussing had any importance for me. If I chanced at any time to express uneasiness about the future, my father would reassure me with the words, "Don't worry, my child. Nothing will happen to us." I never thought I could be so forward as to ask him, "How can you be so sure?" I felt cushioned by the love, reassurance, and protection of my parents, and my fear and apprehension were temporarily assuaged.

My friends were probably as sheltered by their parents as I was, although those with older siblings no doubt heard rumors from them. As I look back upon my childhood and early teen-age years, I realize that I had fewer advantages than I had thought in being an only child, since a parent's protective love closeted one from a sense of alarm. It was as though an artery of information and possible preparation had been cut away, and we were helpless to make a choice, even a futile one!

Being an only child of Hungarian-Jewish parents was even more difficult, since the horrors that had already pierced the lives of Jews in other European countries were still unknown to us; consequently, when they did arrive, these horrors would assault us with fierce rapidity. Even the word *Auschwitz,* I can honestly say, never passed my lips or those of anyone I knew until we were on the train, actually arriving at that destination. And we certainly didn't know its connotation.

One day in the summer of 1943 my father and his two brothers received written orders in the mail to report on a given day to a particular location in order to be taken off to do forced labor. One should remember that all of this was being done by the Hungarian *gendarmerie,* under the authority of the Hungarian government, prior to the German occupation. All of the Jewish men in Hungary who could still work were taken to a central location and then dispersed to various regions.

My father, Uncle Henrik, and Uncle Sany were sent a relatively short distance, to a place near Sarospatak, where Henrik lived. There they did farm work, cultivating the soil. They were not political or military prisoners; they had nothing to do with the war. However, as Jews they were fair game for incarceration.

I remember visiting my father. My mother would pin my name and destination on my jacket. I had to take a horse and buggy ride to the railroad station, then take the local train to Sarospatak. On the farm my father and the other prisoners picked melons (in my mind's eye, I can still see the melons on the ground). I was permitted to visit him about once every two weeks, and I would go with provisions for him from home, particularly food, since he would not permit himself to eat the non-kosher rations given him. My mother did not go with me, since she was obligated to take care of what was left of my father's business and our livestock, as well as to look after my aging and ailing grandmother.

I remember that my mother was both frightened and depressed during my father's absence. She could not be certain he would come back. She harbored in her mind the possibility that he might, at any time, be murdered. All she really had to look forward to were intermittent furloughs, when he would return home briefly, only to be compelled to return to the labor camp.

Each time I made the journey I stayed with my Uncle Henrik's wife and children, and we would all go to see my father and his brothers during the visiting hours. My father said virtually nothing about the conditions of the camp. We never saw the barracks in which he lived. Our visits were confined to the farm area where the men worked. There appeared to be no signs of physical abuse. Yet we were all subject to the fear bred of not knowing the conditions to which they returned each evening. Were they literally in a prison? What were their sleeping conditions? Were they secretly abused and beaten? Above all, we were tormented by the uncertainty of what would happen to them next.

When I visited my father, we discussed family matters, trying to keep a normal flow to the conversation. He maintained his warm and gentle demeanor. He tried as much as possible to smile, as he always had when he spoke with me. These were bittersweet moments, as every reference and every nuance in our conversation was a poignant reminder of joyous hours shared in a world that was coming to an end. He would ask me about my schoolwork and what I did for amusement, and, of course, about my mother.

Probably the lightness of our tone and subject matter and my father's apparent calm was made necessary, to a large degree, by the gendarmes who constantly patrolled the areas where prisoners and their families met on visiting days. Those gendarmes, no doubt, heard what was being said by us and by other families. Who would know today how those prisoners really felt? Who would even know whether they were warned to say nothing on threat of severe punishment? I certainly could not tell.

Every two weeks when I visited my father, I had to miss school for a few days at a time. I couldn't go right home because after meeting with our loved ones, especially my father, I needed consolation in order to calm down from the agitated state in which I found myself. Also, my paternal grandmother had to know that her sons were well and unharmed. Therefore, each visit required a day and one or two overnights away from home with my uncle Henrik's family—all for two precious hours spent with my father.

I later learned that there was a lady named Malvina Cszimadia, who was, to the best of my recollection, a Quaker, and whose picture and description can be found among those of the hundreds of "Righteous Gentiles" whose photos and deeds adorn the walls of the U.S. Holocaust Museum in Washington. She used to gather mail that the men wanted to send home, which she would take with her to be posted. How magnanimous and merciful this small act seems in retrospect when measured against the evils of the time! In the Holocaust Museum I discovered that she lived in Satoraljaujhely. She had awakened one morning to find that a forced labor camp was being erected not far from her house. She decided to help the inmates of that camp and possibly other nearby camps.

Looking back, I am perplexed at our ignorance of what was to come. Very probably the majority of Hungarian Jews would not have believed that their fellow countrymen could engage in organized torture and murder directed at themselves. Had we known, we might have done something to save ourselves. Perhaps it would have been to no avail, but at the very least we would have made the effort. Nothing can satisfactorily explain the silence within our country, and in no way can I fathom the disbelief of Jews like my father, who sheltered their children and themselves from what they could not—or would not—comprehend.

# *The Ghetto*

$M$y father came home from forced labor in the autumn of 1943, when I was fourteen. A few months passed, and during this time he seemed to brood more and more inwardly about some calamity in the making, although he said absolutely nothing to me about it. He was increasingly disillusioned and bewildered by what was taking place around him. As for my mother and me, we were happy, of course, that my father was home, and we did not stop to ask if something worse might be in the making for us.

Early in April 1944 we began our preparations for Passover. As we had every year, we cleaned the house, got rid of the leavened foods, and stored away the utensils that we were forbidden to use on the eight sacred days. My father and I went to pick up the special matzohs we had ordered ahead of time. We cooked and baked and otherwise prepared all the traditional foods of the holiday as though we were living in the most normal of times. The irony that we were preparing to celebrate liberation amid increasing persecution was lost to us.

The Passover of 1944 would be the final period of "normalcy" of my early years, a poignant epilogue to my youth and family and to a stable and centered life. We were, for one last time, together as a family. We had our two seders with the tra-

ditional prayers and food and songs. We attended holiday services in our synagogue, wearing the new clothes we wore every
Passover, as though nothing had changed. By this time, rumors
were already afloat that the Germans had penetrated Budapest.
(The occupation had actually begun on March 19, a month
before.) But despite the trepidation and anguish we felt on
hearing this news, the beauty and tradition of the holiday
comforted us.

On April 16, 1944, a day that will be imbedded in my
memory as long as I live, the gendarmes knocked at our door.
The leader ordered us to leave our homes no later than twenty-
four hours after the time of notification, and to assemble at the
Jewish schoolyard. We would be allowed take along only some
necessary clothing and food. However, we were told to take
with us all our money and jewelry. When we sought to know
where we were going, we were told curtly, "Just follow orders."
We were not stupid or foolhardy. We knew we could question
nothing without the risk of severe punishment. But we sensed
that we would be leaving our homes for a very long time.

We were still in the midst of Passover, as I recall, since we
hadn't yet changed our dishes and cutlery back to what we used
the rest of the year. How grateful I am today that I had even
fourteen years of happy Passovers surrounded by my loving
family! We still had a working farm, and we had all our animals
to care for. We therefore asked our neighbors to come in and
feed the cows and other creatures and to give them water. One
could not simply walk away from live animals. They demanded
responsibility and attention. These neighbors did take on the
responsibility of caring for the animals. But they also appro-
priated everything that belonged to us and other Jews. And
they did it the very day that we were ordered to report to the
schoolyard. No one came with legal papers that gave them a
right to take possession. But they did take possession of our

houses and stores. Our other belongings—were dragged outside and left exposed to the daytime sun, to be purloined and plundered. What we did not lose on the spot was taken from us in the schoolyard on the following day.

April 16, 1944, was the day everything stopped. All the beauty, all the order, all the timeless traditions, all the joys of family life ceased. We now faced a gaping darkness, a terrifying unknown.

As I later learned, we were in Zone 1, one of six "zones," each representing a different geographical area of the country. Our zone was constituted by Carpathio-Ruthenia and Northern Hungary. The population of this zone would later be the first to be transported to Auschwitz. The reason was, very likely, that the Hungarian authorities considered this particular population to be an "alien." or "non-Magyarized" element. It was also the plan of Adolf Eichmann, Hitler's right-hand man in Hungary, to keep the Jews of Budapest, who were the most "sophisticated" and "assimilated" in Hungary, in the dark as long as possible so that they could not escape into the countryside to hide. The Budapest Jews in Zone 6 were the last to be taken.

On the very next day we reported to the schoolyard, as we had been ordered. All families had to register when they got there. We were told curtly and emphatically, "Hand over all of your valuables, especially money and jewelry. You're not going to need it, since you're going to be resettled. Just follow orders." I wanted to ask them, although I would never have dared to say it aloud, "How is it that you know where I'm going, and I don't?"

However, there was absolutely no resistance or attempt to evade the orders given. One was too petrified to question or disobey the gendarmes unless one wished to risk life and limb in a beating or even worse. The gendarmes knew who was Jewish, of course, because for almost a full year we had been forced to wear yellow Stars of David on our clothing. One had only to point a finger at one of us ("There comes a Jew!") for us to experience humiliation and, even worse, brutality. We had been devalued, dehumanized, and persecuted.

At the schoolyard we waited for the inhabitants of the smaller towns around Tolcsva to assemble. Meanwhile our belongings, which we were never to see again, were being placed upon wagons owned and driven not by strangers, but by neighbors and long-time friends, people with whom my father had done business. My father was shocked to see one of his lifelong friends, with whom he had served in the First World War, driving one of the wagons. I was shocked and saddened that the people who had known my parents most of their lives, and whom we had regarded at the very least as neighbors, were helping themselves to whatever portable possessions they could manage to take from our houses. They also voluntarily and cheerfully helped the authorities to get rid of us Jews, marching us from our homes to the schoolyard and then to a ghetto, an enclosed area where we would live apart from them, deprived of all comforts and of even our basic needs. And few offered a word of sympathy or consolation.

From the schoolyard we proceeded to Satoraljaujhely, which was to serve as our ghetto. Mothers with infants and the elderly, including my grandmother, were permitted to ride. The rest of us were forced to go on foot. We walked nonstop for a day and a half. My mother had spent the full twenty-four hours we had been given to leave our homes preparing food for us to eat along the way: smoked goose, cheese, and hard-boiled eggs. We ate hungrily, perhaps realizing that provisions would be scant from now on. We found out later that we were right, since in the ghetto all food was rationed severely.

When we finally got to the ghetto, we saw the other members of our family who lived in our region, Zemplen Megye. Satoraljaujhely was the county seat of the region and its largest metropolis. The ghetto was situated in a dilapidated area of the city near the railroad station, a fact that at the time had little significance for me. However, this was not the station where luxury trains came in, the trains that transported people on business or on holiday. That station was in the middle of the town. To our station, as we would later realize, came the freight trains that transported a very different kind of cargo: human beings destined for annihilation. Gypsies had lived in this part of town before being driven out by the Hungarian authorities. They, too, would soon be targets of mass murder.

The ghetto was to be closed off from the outside world, but I remember that at the gate we encountered two of our gentile neighbors, members of the Kovacs family, who brought us some provisions, embraced my mother, and expressed their sorrow for what was happening to us. However, they were the only ones who did so. I don't remember their given names today, but I remember the sorrow and pity in their faces and the way my mother wept.

One of the few consolations my family had in the ghetto was that we were all in the same place and could care for each other. As long as I had my mother and father, I felt protected. As a child who was close to her extended family, I found some pleasure and comfort in the fact that my cousins, my aunts and uncles, and I could still be near one another in the ghetto. We saw each other constantly. We sat, talked, prayed, and reminisced. However, we never discussed "concentration camps," a term with which we were hardly familiar. While we were there, no one spoke of the future; we clung as much as was possible to our past. Whatever bleak thoughts parents or other adults harbored were kept to themselves.

We were in the ghetto for only a few weeks. Our provisions were meager. As many people as could be were placed in a single room. There were no fewer than ten people in a room, many of them strangers to one another. Our room was lit by a kerosene lamp. We had no electricity, no plumbing, and no heating. We slept on the floor, on mattresses stuffed with straw. However, there was a laundry, so we washed our clothes regularly and tried to keep as clean as we could under the circumstances. We tried also to cook the little food we had. Food was rationed to each family, and we made the best of the situation. A group of us would pool our food and make something consisting of the pooled ingredients. Our family—aunts, uncles, cousins—used to eat together. Whoever had more of a certain food item would divide it among the whole group.

Our rations were so meager that I was perpetually hungry. I was unused to being without food, and I kept thinking and talking about my mother's ample and delicious meals from the past. I had particularly loved her fried chicken. She had managed to salvage a jar containing some chicken fat, and one of the "luxuries" of my existence at that time was for my mother to take some bread and fry it in melted chicken fat, so that the bread resembled fried chicken. I would proceed to devour it ravenously, with eyes closed, imagining myself devouring fried chicken. To me, at that time, this was the most delectable of treats. Although I am not in the same condition today as I was in the ghetto, when I am alone at home, I still sometimes fry a piece of bread in chicken fat and eat it. In that way I feel a closeness to my mother.

We had no hygienic facilities. There was one outhouse for our section of the ghetto, and it was to serve everyone. (Each section of the ghetto had about a thousand people; the population of the entire ghetto was around four thousand.) However, the children, including me, were told not to go there early in the morning because the outhouse had to be "cleaned up." During our time in the ghetto, many suicides took place in the outhouse. Several people, who perhaps knew or sensed what was going to happen and found it impossible to face their fears, slashed their throats or wrists there in the early hours of the morning. We children were not allowed to go to the outhouse, no matter how extreme our need; we had to use the potties in the rooms until they cleaned out these outhouses, because the adults didn't want the children to see the bloody residue of self-slaughter.

Around us was a terrible sense of aimlessness and desperation. Life seemed to have lost its purpose during those agonizing days. People tried to survive amid oppression, hunger, illness, loss of dignity, and loss of faith. I still carry with me the memory of men standing around all day, wearing their prayer shawls and phylacteries, perpetually praying to God. I would ask myself what they were praying for. Was it rescue? Was it release through a merciful death?

So sheltered had been my existence, and so much had I taken for granted the comfortable and well-insulated life of a dearly loved only child, that I found it terribly difficult to sustain the deprivations of those weeks in the ghetto. Those weeks, which in retrospect were comparatively few and were far from the worst part of my experience, became my initiation into a new life, a life that was to be overwhelmingly shocking and terrifying.

One of the most difficult aspects of ghetto life to adjust to was its utter boredom and purposelessness. To the best of my recollection, we had no set routine. We started each morning washing ourselves at a basin, which my family had to share with the other families in our room, after which we proceeded to say our morning prayers. Then we had some meager portions of bread, or an egg if one was available, or some cheese if we could find a morsel, and some tea. If there was enough milk, the very young children were given it. Usually we were assigned some cleaning jobs around the ghetto, or perhaps some tasks in the laundry. The men and the older teenagers, both boys and girls, were taken to clean the streets of Satoraljaujhely with large brooms. I am certain that this was done mainly to demean the Jews before the gentiles. The younger children among us stayed and helped our grandmothers and mothers. We socialized as best we could with the other ghetto children. I amused myself with my cousins and with many friends from Tolcsva. This was the most pleasure we Jews could hope for and the most tolerable part of our sojourn in the ghetto. We behaved well, with decorum and restraint, because we knew in our hearts that something was deeply wrong and that we might be at the threshold of some final upheaval.

We were under the "leadership" of a *Judenrat,* or Jewish council (in Hungarian, *Zsido hitkoszeg*), but the real authorities were the Hungarian gendarmes, who constantly watched us, and who mocked, tormented, and abused the Jewish populace of the ghetto. The municipal authorities, including the mayor, sanctioned the brutalities, at the very least. The mayor of Satoraljaujhely, Indar Varo, and the captain of the *gendarmerie* were condemned to death after the war. It must never be forgotten that the cruelty we had endured to this point stemmed not from the Germans, but from the indigenous population of Hungarians, as there was never a single German visible in the ghetto.

Many Jews, of course, had no idea of what awaited them, and believed that their ghettoization was "precautionary" because of military operations in the area. There were some "oversights" by the Hungarians of the usual restrictions set by the German authorities. These oversights took advantage of our ignorance. For example, Hungarian-Jewish children under the age of ten were exempted from wearing the yellow Star of David; however, they were not to be exempted from deportation and eventual murder. The gendarmes treated them as it did their elders. Jewish men still attached to military labor units were taken also, though these military labor units were considered indispensable to the nation.

Only two circumstances made the ghetto bearable for me. My father had there a Jewish friend with whom he had served in the First World War. To him he had pledged that, if both survived that war and had children of opposite sexes, those children would become betrothed. This was commonplace in Orthodox Jewish communities of the time. My father's friend had a son, and this young man was in the ghetto with us. He was seventeen or eighteen, and I was fourteen. My father reiterated the pledge to this young man. The young man begged my father to let us marry then and there. My father refused, saying that times were too uncertain in the ghetto, but that if both of us survived the war, we would then surely be able to marry. I survived, but the young man did not. I found out after my liberation that he had been killed in one of the camps. But his presence in the ghetto made the experience more bearable for me.

The other thing that made the ghetto bearable for me was the incessant throb of memory of joyous times in our agricultural community, with its simple natural pleasures, and of family life surrounded by the beauty of our traditions. Memory of that life, and yearning for reattachment to that life, however futile, somehow kept me going.

On May 25, 1944, little more than a month after our arrival, we boarded a train to leave Satoraljaujhely, bound for what we thought was a labor camp. We were certain no harm would come to us. As I have mentioned, there was a Jewish council, and an elder was chosen by the Germans to direct us. In our ghetto the head of the council was a man named Lapy Klein. He was under the jurisdiction of the gendarmes, and he was powerless to do anything but spur us on. Earlier he had been responsible for the welfare of the poor. He had supervised charities in the Jewish community. None of us doubted his sincerity or his loyalty to the community. When he instructed us, his anguish was visible on his face. There is no doubt that his heart was breaking even as he spoke.

As we proceeded to the train, I walked between my parents, holding onto their hands. My grandmother walked on the other side of my mother. Aunts, uncles, and cousins walked behind us. This was to be our final walk together on Hungarian soil.

Suddenly I saw my first German officer, dressed in an immaculate uniform and brimming with authority. Beside him was a fearsome police dog. I feared to look up at the officer. I could only hear his voice barking orders at us in his language. I began to whimper.

# Auschwitz

$A$s I recall today our departure from the ghetto, I feel a terrible bitterness. I ask myself the question, "Where was the free world, and why did they not do something to prevent or limit the deportation and mass slaughter of human beings?" Since the Hungarian Jews were the last to be taken to the death camps of Poland, could not the United States and the Allies have done something to prevent the machinery of death from grinding away? Were they so helpless or so ignorant, by this time, of the barbarities that they could not bomb the railroad tracks to Auschwitz? The Allied military was undoubtedly well briefed by now on the Final Solution. I doubt that I will ever understand the failure of the Allies to respond to the evil perpetrated at this time.

The Germans were now taking over from the Hungarians. We heard shouts, "*Macht schnell! Raus! Raus!*" (Go fast! Beat it! Scram!) Police dogs were used to spur us on into the cattle cars in which we were to spend the next several miserable days. There were eighty to one hundred men, women, and children packed into each car.

Four transports left Satoraljaujhely that day; we were on the third. The Hungarian gendarmes were callous to the end, humiliating, mocking, and abusing us. People were attacked with truncheons and bullwhips for any minor infraction or slow movement. Although it did not happen to us personally, other eyewitnesses claimed that people leaving Satoraljaujhely were degraded by means of body searches and that many had all personal documents and means of identification taken from them, thus turning them immediately into "nonpersons," as they were shoved onto the trains. Ironically, the Nazis made a film documentary in which they attempted to show Hungarian brutality toward Jewish deportees, in contrast to their own "civility."

From the region of Zemplen Megye fifteen thousand Jews were deported, and only two hundred and fifty survived. From my own family sixty-eight were deported, and only two survived.

I can hardly begin to describe the horror of the train ride to our destination. The railroad car into which we were herded was normally used for cattle or freight. At least eighty people were thrown together in my car with no regard for age or infirmity. There was nowhere for us to sit. We had two pails, one at either end of each car, to be used as bathroom facilities. We were expected to empty out the pails at each station stop. At each stop there was someone who ladled water to those on the train who were fortunate enough to be close to the door, where they could get some. I was not lucky enough to be that close. If anyone in our family was able to get ahold of the ladle with the water, that person shared the contents with other family members, so that each one got a drop of water.

It wasn't long before whatever food any of us possessed ran out. None of us had enough to sustain us. Each time we stopped in a new town we took on a new engineer, and tolls had to be paid to get through. The voyage was agonizingly slow and lengthy. I remember infants screaming, usually from hunger and thirst. Their mothers were without the resources to feed them, not even a bit of milk, and in desperation some strangled their babies to quiet them and free themselves of the unbearable torment of being able to do nothing.

I heard and saw a lot of crying, a lot of praying. I heard people screaming, "Blood is spilling all over!" Some people had taken their lives on the train. Once in a while I saw blood gushing in the cattle car as people committed suicide, using a knife or a razor blade. When something like this happened, my mother or father tried to protect me, to shield me from the horror. "Stay in the corner. Everything is all right. Everything is all right!" they would say to soothe my terror. I held onto my mother and father and grandmother for dear life. I was still only fourteen. With their gentle voices they tried to relax me and make me go to sleep, even though there was no place to sit or squat. I am certain I fell asleep here or there, even in a standing position. One gets used to certain noises, and simply dozes off.

The dead were not taken from the train. The ones who were bleeding simply lay there. The smells of blood and corpses and waste matter went into our nostrils. All kinds of smells mingled through those cattle cars.

It was well into the month of May. Summer was already on the horizon. Sometimes I would try to make my way to the narrow slits through which I hoped to glimpse a fragment of light. From time to time we wondered where we were. Were we out of Hungary yet? Where were they taking us? I would see only fragments of sunlight and greenery. The trees were by now adorned with leaves, and flowers were pushing through the spring soil, signs of a world flourishing with life. At the same time, our world seemed to be approaching its desperate and bitter end.

We were finally arriving at our destination: Auschwitz.

One had to marvel at the ingenious and demonic planning of the Nazis, at their ability to deceive all of us. Most of us were not yet at the stage of dehumanization where we could con-ceive of being totally separated from our families and from every connection to the world we had known. Just before the train stopped for the last time, signifying our arrival at the camp, we passed small rows of houses that I could observe through the slits in the freight car. I glimpsed a benign scene of flowers growing, children playing, and members of family units interacting. This sight made me feel, as it would prob-ably have made anyone feel, that our life was to be like this. A deceptive ray of hope! I am certain that if the International Red Cross had ever visited Auschwitz, these scenes are what they would have seen on the way. Had they gone past the iron gate with its deceptive inscription, "*Arbeit Macht Frei*" (Work will free you), they would have seen a different world: a hell beyond the human powers of depiction.

Never in our wildest dreams did we think we were going into a camp to be slaughtered. Never! I cannot forgive the free world for not allowing the Hungarian Jews to know what was going on. We weren't privy to anything. There had been no reports, not even leaflets dropped from the sky. Yes, some under-ground people had tried to warn the Jews of Budapest, but they were not believed. They were not believed because the Jews had had no prior exposure to what was truly taking place. Had information been available before the Jews were deported and taken to their slaughter, I am almost certain there would have been some kind of protest, some kind of resistance, some attempt to hide, even some effort on the part of the Hungarian non-Jewish population to help us. Perhaps I'm wrong, but I have to have some faith in the human race!

When we arrived at the camp, the doors of the train were quickly slid open, and we were driven out by *kapos* (camp foremen), all Polish, and many of them Jews. The German S.S. didn't "soil" their hands with this flotsam and jetsam of humanity; they merely barked out orders: "*Schnell! Schnell! Raus! Raus!*" The *kapos* were usually physically more powerful than the Germans. Some were truly brutal, but others showed a touch of compassion.

The cattle cars were high off the ground. There was no stepladder for us to get down on. One had to jump down, whether old or young, ill or well. Those who couldn't jump were pulled or dragged by the *kapos*. The *kapos* had to do this; they could not do otherwise or they would have been beaten or killed. Some apologized while they were doing it; some even had tears in their eyes. I saw my elderly grandmothers pulled off the train right before my eyes. We were forced to leave our few remaining belongings in the cattle car. The *kapos* tried to reassure us with the lie that we would soon see our belongings.

The moment we got off the train, we knew we had entered hell. Immediately the Germans began screaming: "Get in line! Men and women separate, then march forward in rows of five!" We marched forward. We were now moving toward what was known as Auschwitz II: Birkenau (Birch Grove), whose name was deceptively pleasant for a killing center. When it had first been built in the winter of 1941–42, Jews had had to debark from the trains a distance from Birkenau and walk or be trucked to the place where they would be "selected" for life or death. In the few months before our arrival, in anticipation of a huge influx of Hungarian Jews, the rail line had been extended to Birkenau so that the process of human disposal could be achieved more quickly and efficiently.

When the men were ordered to stand on one side and the women on the other, my father stood with his two brothers, his brother-in-law, and several cousins. I stood with my mother, grandmother, aunts, and young female cousins. I was holding on tightly to my mother's hand. At one point, my father broke out of the line of men and ran over to me. I never expected him to do such a thing. I was in a state of shock. I will not forget this moment as long as I live. His face was snow-white, and he put his hands on either side of my head. As he did this, he uttered a blessing in Hebrew, in the same manner as he did on every Sabbath eve: "May God give you the blessings of Sarah, Rebecca, Rachel, and Leah." He cautioned me to look after myself, whatever happened, and to be "a good girl." For this he was seized by German soldiers and beaten mercilessly before my eyes, and then pulled back in line while the beating continued. He never had the chance to say goodbye to his wife or his female relatives! Soon he, like so many others, was to be taken away. My last sight of him was as he stood in line, bent over from the blows he had received, blood streaming down his face.

I continued holding onto my mother's hand as we walked along a ramp. Suddenly, there loomed before me a huge figure. The image burned itself into my brain. As I later learned, it belonged to Dr. Josef Mengele, known to the prisoners as "the angel of death." He stood before us—tall and handsome, wearing shiny leather boots, leather trousers, a leather jacket, and immaculate white gloves. I shivered in absolute terror as I looked at him. He brandished a stick as might an orchestra conductor wielding a baton. A huge dog stood at his side.

With his stick, Mengele played God. He pointed either to the left or to the right, thus determining who would live and who would die. We were to find out, all too soon, that if he pointed to the left one went to the work camp. If he pointed to the right, one's ultimate fate was the crematorium. Suddenly my mother's hand was torn away from mine. Eventually my mother, my grandmother, one of my mother's sisters-in-law, and my two young cousins were taken away to what, I later realized, was the gas chamber. The separation was so abrupt that my mother was not able to hear my crying. We never said goodbye. That was the last time I saw my mother, grandmother, and those other relatives who had been so dear to me. I was sent to the left with my father's sister, Elizabeth, and her sister-in-law, Sarika Grunhut, whom I called Sari.

I became numb; I couldn't hear, couldn't see. My Aunt Elizabeth and Sari pulled me along. We were soon sent to the other side of the camp. As we were walking along, a chance meeting virtually decided my fate. Not far from the barbed wire, we saw a distant cousin from my father's family, who must have been in the previous transport, and she gestured to us. Speaking quietly enough that the *kapos* would not hear and pointing to me, she told my aunt, "When you're registered, lie about her age. Say that she is eighteen rather than fourteen, so that the Germans won't send her back to the crematorium." It was the first time I had heard "crematorium," and quite naturally I did not know to what it referred. From that point on, I was thought to be eighteen.

Along with the other young women from our transport who had been deemed "fit" for labor, and thereby for at least temporary life, my aunt, Sari, and I were brought to an enormous room where we were ordered to disrobe. One could scarcely imagine the feeling that came from being one of thousands who, naked, were scarcely recognizable or distinguishable. Our clothes were stacked in piles; skirts, dresses, underclothes, sleepwear, all that was personal, disappeared from our possession in mountainous heaps. Then *kapos* began shaving our hair with huge clippers. Almost unconsciously, I began crying out for my mother. My aunt grabbed me, covered my mouth, quietly admonished me for crying, and finally succeeded in calming me down.

We were then completely shorn. For the first time, I broke down in terror. I was shocked as I saw myself reflected in the other beings before me. We were nude and shaven. I gasped as I perceived how depersonalized we had become. We were now truly unrecognizable to each other!

Each of us was issued a prison uniform made from potato sack material, and a pair of wooden shoes, and marched outside. No attempt was made to issue clothing in accordance with one's shape or size. It was as though we were to be deprived of any semblance of identity or dignity.

Although I did not know it at the time, the room we had been in was a gassing center. I had noticed showerheads in the ceiling and had believed that indeed that was what they were. On my return to Auschwitz a few months later, I learned that the "showerheads" actually emitted Zyklon B, the poison gas developed by the Nazis that was used to murder so many human beings. If there were not too many transports, the new arrivals would be gassed in those rooms and then taken to the crematoria. I also later found peepholes in the wall through which the S.S. could watch the Jews being gassed.

After leaving this room we were made to stand for hours in line as we were counted and endlessly recounted. The Germans were notorious for keeping prisoners in line for hours at a time. This agonizing process would recur with monotonous regularity over the following weeks and months. It mattered not whether there was rain, heat, snow, or blistering cold. The *Zahlappell* (roll call) continued. Why we had to submit to the roll call I shall never know. Did the S.S. honestly believe we had even the remotest possibility of escaping? Any attempt at uprising would have met with violent retaliation. Any effort to escape would have been reciprocated with a bullet from an S.S. guard on the watchtower or with electrocution at the barbed wire fence. There was no hesitation about killing prisoners.

This was the wet season in Poland. Thus we were forced to endure exposure during hours of incessant rain. The prisoners stood there shivering, numb, praying for some help, but we got no relief. If one of us fell from hunger, exhaustion, or bodily weakness, that prisoner was pulled out of line. Whether she was sent to the infirmary or directly to execution we never knew. What we did come to know with absolute certainty was that we would never see her again.

We gradually lost all sense of time. We were assigned to our barracks. Each barrack was a long building on either side of which were planks on several levels that were serving as bunk beds. In the center of the barrack was a brick divider. We crawled into our bunks and waited for the next order. That order was to get down and stand in line for a piece of hard bread and watery soup which had dirty vegetation floating in it, if anything at all.

Later we had "lights out." As many prisoners as could be were placed alongside each other, and we slept five abreast. (Virtually everything we were ordered to do was done in groups of five.) No one could turn to one side or another, so congested was our sleeping space. When we were awakened, it was still dark. Outside the barrack was an ersatz "bathroom" in the style of an outhouse. The "bathroom facilities" consisted of wooden boards with holes cut in them. There were pipes with water dribbling out of them. One could never relieve oneself when the need was there. One had to wait for specific times, and then one could never go alone. We had to stand in a line of from thirty to fifty people. If a prisoner dawdled or stopped to talk to someone, she was whipped by one of the S.S. women who guarded us. The lines were required to be in constant motion.

The female S.S. in Auschwitz were even more brutal to us than the males, who "merely" kicked us or hit us with their truncheons. The women showed their authority and cruelty far more regularly and enthusiastically than did the men, man-handling us at every opportunity They degraded us regularly and dug their nails into our flesh, using phrases like "*Judenschwein*" (Jewish pig) and "Jewish whore" and spitting on us.

Following another interminable roll call and a meager breakfast of watery coffee and a hardened crust of bread, we were set to work cleaning the barrack or doing some other menial chores. At noontime we stood in line in rows of five for our "meal" of watery soup and a crust of hard black bread. Anyone attempting to go back for more was severely beaten.

When I say we lost all sense of time, I mean that for days on end, either life seemed utterly purposeless or my brain simply blotted out any sense of sequence or logical continuity. I can close my eyes and see what everything looked like, yet I can remember nothing that had meaning. That first time in Auschwitz, I remember a sense of numbness; it is probable that for many of us, it was simply a matter of waiting for the end. Many of us believed, and do to this day, that our captors gave us something in our food that dehumanized us by turning us into automatons. We were not functioning as normal beings. This was my induction into hell. I lost all sense of free will.

# 6

# A Closer Look at Hell

To us, remaining alive meant being mobile. My Aunt Elizabeth, Sari, and I did not remain in Auschwitz long. After approximately six weeks in Birkenau, in June we were sent with several hundred other girls and women to Cracow as part of a "work brigade." We were put on a train that was not nearly as congested as the one that had brought us to Auschwitz. We even felt a certain elation; after all, nothing could have been worse than what we had already experienced. Our spirits had been broken by the sudden and terrible losses we had endured. Although we knew nothing of our family's fate, we suspected the worst. But at least the three of us were together.

Once we arrived in Cracow, we were put on military trucks. We rode in the midst of wind and rain, with no covering over our heads. As we went through the town I observed "normal" people walking through the streets and seeing "real" houses with people living in them. I wondered if we were all living on the same planet. Finally, we arrived at a camp called Plaszow. There were mountains in the background and a circle of barracks surrounding a square. We did not know what to expect next. On the surface it appeared to be a better place than Auschwitz. How wrong we were!

I do not know exactly what purpose our labor in Plaszow served, except to heighten the level of sadism within our persecutors Nevertheless, our barrack was more bearable. There, too, I remember that we were awakened when it was still dark outside, and we were forced to stand for two or three hours while we were counted and recounted. One thing that did not vary was the *Zahlappell!*

During the day our labor force was sent to a stone quarry. Our jobs consisted of chiseling stones out of a wall, lifting them, and putting them on a lorry, which we had to push from one end of the quarry to the other. If anyone dropped a stone or slowed down in work or failed to lift a heavy enough stone, she was assaulted mercilessly by the S.S. with bayonets or was attacked by police dogs. The police dogs would jump on the prisoner, tear at her clothes, and bite into her flesh.

While working up the mountainsides we could look down into the valley where the barracks were. Often we saw people assembled in the middle of the square where our barrack stood. These people were not dressed as prisoners. They wore street clothes and were, we assumed, political prisoners. As they stood in line, they were methodically machine-gunned. This sight recurred frequently during our time in Plaszow. Once the bodies were removed, what was left was a bloodbath. When we returned in the evening from our work detail, we were forced to clean up the dried blood in the square. We were given brushes with which to do the cleaning. The Germans sprayed the ground with water from a hose both before and after, and sometimes they even sprayed us while we were scrubbing.

The S.S. played a "hunting game" with us in Cracow. The game, known as "decimation," was used to terrify and desensitize us. We were lined up in rows every morning. As the Germans proceeded down the line, they counted from one to ten and shot every tenth person. I do not know how or why I

escaped being that tenth person, as did my aunt and Sari. Once
I was right next to one who was shot, and the precariousness
of the circumstance still sends a terrifying shiver up and down
my spine. Some of us were actually praying, "Let me be next.
Take me out of my misery. I've had enough!" Some would say
that God had a mission for certain people, such as me, because
we were still alive. Yet my doubts remain with me. What about
the others? Did they deserve to suffer and die? I still ask myself
why God turned away from His people to allow such a ruthless
and capricious slaughter.

The person shot would fall down bleeding, and we were
allowed to do nothing to help. One who has not experienced
it cannot truly understand the torture and the horror of standing by, unable to do anything, fearing that one would be the
next person killed, or of seeing someone else, perhaps a friend
or a loved one, mercilessly shot down and feeling guilty to have
survived. We simply watched, petrified and frozen.

After the "game" we had to pick up the bodies and load
them onto trucks, and the Germans would dump them into mass
trenches. Some of the women in the trenches were still alive
and crying out as fresh bodies were dumped on top of them.
Soil was shoveled in to cover them, and that was the end of it.

For that reason alone, I could not today visit a concentration camp. How could I walk on that soil? I would not know
whose grave, whose blood, whose flesh I would be walking on.
I could never go back to those camps! Never!

In Cracow, as in Birkenau, breakfast was made up of black
water, which the S.S. called "coffee," and a piece of hard brown
bread. Then our captors would take us to the quarry, where we
worked all day. We were counted when we went out the gates;
we were counted when we came back in. Then we'd get our
dinner: watery soup with some hard bread. Also as at Birkenau,
there were things in the soup, such as dirty cabbage leaves, with

green worms swimming around the leaves. Sometimes one even found batches of hair in the soup. But we ignored these things. We pushed them aside, and we ate. Why did we eat? Was it just to keep from starving? I can speak only for myself. Perhaps I ate because my aunt was forcing me, saying, "You must eat! You must eat!" Certainly if I had not eaten, I would have weakened and eventually died. I ask myself, "Could I have mentally sunk to the level where I, the once finicky child who often rejected her mother's food, would devour this gruesome mess?" I can't even rationalize this today, except in terms of an animal life force that simply propelled me away from the thought of suicide by starvation.

One morning in early August, instead of going to work we stayed longer at *Zahlappell*. Suddenly we saw army trucks. They stopped, and we were ordered to board them. Our caravan started out of Plaszow. We were brought to the railroad station in Cracow, where we had to wait for several hours. The sun was beating down on us. I was remembering the day nearly two months before when we had arrived in Cracow in a chilly rain. Now the summer heat was unbearable. There we stood, sickly, broken in body, starved, parched from thirst, and exposed to the relentless August sun.

Finally the freight train arrived, and we were ordered to board. "One hundred to a car!" the S.S. man shouted. One hundred to a car that could not hold half that number! We nearly suffocated from the heat and the smell of one another. I felt my Aunt Elizabeth becoming more and more faint. I kept looking in vain for a place in the corner of the cattle car where she could find some air. The train remained stationary for an eternity. Other trucks arrived, and more women were pushed into our car. We were so packed together that we could not move our arms or legs. People kept falling against each other. Some were even knocked to the floor.

Suddenly I panicked. My aunt and Sari had disappeared from my view! Where were they? It took several long minutes of trying to stretch in the limited space I had before I could find them again. We had been pushed a distance from each other.

By nightfall the train had not yet moved. Finally, to our relief, the train began to jerk forward. One cannot know what our terror was like. We felt much more vulnerable in a fixed position, as when the train was still. As long as the train was in motion, we felt we could cling to life. None of us knew where we were being taken, but at this point did it matter?

So our stay in Plaszow was over, leaving us much more "enlightened" about sudden death and the vulnerability of our lives. Now just fifteen, I had seen people tortured, arbitrarily shot. And it had changed me. I had learned that one could exist amid fear, hunger, abuse. I had learned to eat worms, and I had grown calluses on my young hands. I was far thinner when I left Plaszow than when I had left Auschwitz a few weeks earlier. It no longer mattered how I lived; it mattered only *that* I lived. My last remnant of sheltered youth evaporated in Plaszow.

The train took us back to Auschwitz. I was only four months older than the healthy and active young girl who had been driven into the ghetto with her family, but I was like an automaton. I followed orders and did what the S.S. told me to do every day. I no longer worried about the consequences of things. But I was already wiser, less innocent. I knew exactly what the smoke meant, what the chimneys were for. I knew that the Germans were burning human flesh, that people were being turned into ashes. The odor of burning flesh was unmistakable and unbearable. It entered us through our nostrils and burned our eyes. I knew that the people who were being turned into charcoal were transports, as I had been in what seemed like centuries ago. Now the realization of what had happened to my parents, my grandmothers, my aunts and uncles, and my younger cousins assaulted me vividly.

I also received my tattoo during my second time in Auschwitz. My number is A22029 (the "A" stands for Auschwitz). I call it one of Hitler's footsteps on my body. Many of my fellow survivors have removed theirs, but I have decided that I am going to die with mine.

I was given a job during this period of time in Auschwitz: working in the kitchen. Actually one could hardly have called it a kitchen. It was a huge room that resembled a canvass-covered tent. There was a gigantic kettle under which we lit a fire. That was where the "cooks" made their so–called soups and coffees, where they threw everything, clean or unclean, that they could find, whatever "vegetable," edible or inedible. Sometimes I found a brush or a comb in there. My job was to clean the kettle. I was given a damp cloth with which to wipe it. To keep the kettle clean, I needed a faucet and running water. But I never had access to those. However, I had one advantage over the other prisoners: I could pick the remnants from the kettle with my fingers. This provided me with added "nourishment" and strength. Had I been caught, I would surely have been beaten or killed. However, like all surviving prisoners, I had reached a level at which survival in nearly any form had become acceptable and worth any risk.

One day my Aunt Elizabeth and I received a brutal beating and had to kneel on hard corn kernels for hours because she had sneaked back into the line at my urging in order to get a little extra nourishment for herself. Though my intention had been to help her sustain what little strength she had, I felt terribly guilty because her suffering was a result of my prompting her. However, she said nothing, refusing in any way to blame me.

The few tranquil moments we were able to seize in Auschwitz came from the recollections we nurtured of an earlier and happier time, particularly the memories of the meals we had shared outdoors during harvest time in Tolcsva. Ironically, though, that which made life momentarily bearable was what was no longer attainable: the simple pleasures of the bucolic life we had once enjoyed amid the beauty of nature and the serene presence of loved ones.

At every moment I was forcibly reminded of the fragility of life and of the need to hold onto it by whatever means possible, disregarding how temporary that life might be. I saw what happened to girls I knew. At one point, I recall, a friend of mine recognized her mother on the other side of the barbed wire. Simultaneously, her mother recognized her. They naturally ran toward each other. As each one touched the electrified fence in her zeal to reach the other, both were instantly electrocuted.

I realized during my second stay in Auschwitz that most of the good-looking Hungarian girls and women were no longer with us because they had been taken away forcibly upon arrival to serve as camp prostitutes. What happened to them, how many survived and how, I shall never know. I knew some of them from the ghetto. I can imagine what they went through and how they were treated. More than likely, the Germans did not want the nature of that treatment to be exposed to the outside world.

During our second sojourn in Auschwitz the barracks seemed different from those we had been in earlier. They were much larger and longer, more crowded with inmates. We were each given an army blanket, nothing else. Once more we slept on wooden planks, five in a row. When we went out for *Zahlappell*, we could see barracks like ours for miles on end. We saw many inmates, both men and women, walking on the roads, followed by S.S. guards. I assumed they were coming and going from their work assignments.

After a while we were deadened to everything but the effort to survive another day. We were so dehumanized that our powers of resistance virtually disappeared. We felt ourselves to be less than human. No one in my group thought of rebelling. We never knew for certain, but most of us suspected that something had been put in our food to keep us from menstruating. (We know now what we didn't know then: that menstruation stops when the body is subjected to stress.) It seemed as though the Nazis wanted nothing less than the authority to deprive us of our biological functions, our sense of womanliness, and our normal instincts and feelings.

During my second stay in Auschwitz, I also became aware of the other things that were going on, things that involved the infamous Dr. Josef Mengele. We had heard of the twins into whose eyes he had injected dyes to change eye color, the surgical removal of fingers from one twin and the grafting of them to the other. We heard also of the torture of pregnant women and the ripping of fetuses from their bodies. As hardened as we had become to the bizarre and savage unreality of everyday life in Auschwitz, we still found the sadistically performed horrors we heard about revolting.

That we had not yet lost our sense of revulsion gave us a certain reassurance that we still retained a spark of life, however small. I am not sure about all the others, but some of my fellow inmates and I still continued to believe in a Divine Presence, which manifested itself amid the hell in which we were forced to live. We still remembered the Jewish holidays, and somehow, despite being deprived of calendars, we could track them and observe them to the best of our ability.

It was all inexplicable to us, yet I can still remember how we stood in line for food on Yom Kippur, the Day of Atonement on which Jews normally fast and pray. We resolved not to eat, despite the fact that on any "normal" day we subsisted on less than a thousand calories and knew starvation and hunger intimately. Those who fasted still remembered the Biblical covenant with God, and they would not betray their faith though they lived with daily despair.

Why, then did we bother to stand in line? Perhaps so that we would have a little more food for the next day. Perhaps, even more significantly, so that the Germans would not assume that we were giving them permission to cut our rations even more because we had chosen to fast on this holiest of days.

.

The Granat family: left to right, Minna (Margit's aunt), Bertha
(her grandmother), Danis (her uncle), Odon (her grandfather),
and Theresa (her mother).

Joseph Buchhalter
(Margit's father)
during World War I.

Wedding picture of Margit's parents, Theresa and Joseph Buchhalter,
August 20, 1928.

Margit (right), age 5, with her cousin Edith, age 4, and paternal grandmother, Lina Buchhalter.

The synagogue in Tolcsva before World War II.

Margit's aunt, Elizabeth Grunhut, who died in Bergen-Belsen.

The S.S. *Drottingholm*, the ship that brought Margit to America in 1946.

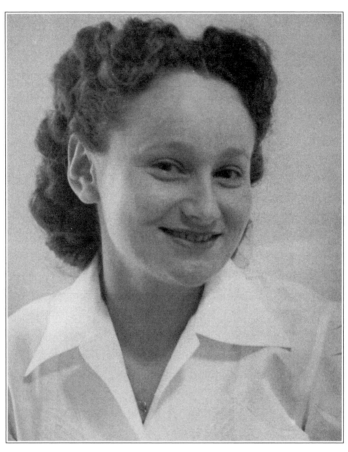

Margit as an X-ray technician in America, 1951.

Wedding picture of Margit and Harvey Feldman, December 13, 1953.

Courtyard of Margit's home in Tolcsva on her return in 1972. Pictured are the residents at the time and Margit's uncle Henrick Buchhalter, facing camera at right.

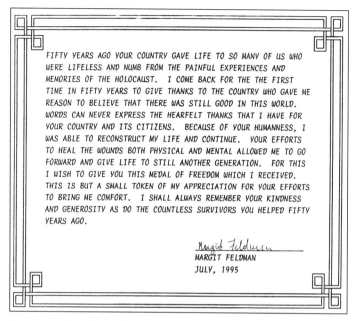

FIFTY YEARS AGO YOUR COUNTRY GAVE LIFE TO SO MANY OF US WHO
WERE LIFELESS AND NUMB FROM THE PAINFUL EXPERIENCES AND
MEMORIES OF THE HOLOCAUST. I COME BACK FOR THE THE FIRST
TIME IN FIFTY YEARS TO GIVE THANKS TO THE COUNTRY WHO GAVE ME
REASON TO BELIEVE THAT THERE WAS STILL GOOD IN THIS WORLD.
WORDS CAN NEVER EXPRESS THE HEARFELT THANKS THAT I HAVE FOR
YOUR COUNTRY AND ITS CITIZENS. BECAUSE OF YOUR HUMANNESS, I
WAS ABLE TO RECONSTRUCT MY LIFE AND CONTINUE. YOUR EFFORTS
TO HEAL THE WOUNDS BOTH PHYSICAL AND MENTAL ALLOWED ME TO GO
FORWARD AND GIVE LIFE TO STILL ANOTHER GENERATION. FOR THIS
I WISH TO GIVE YOU THIS MEDAL OF FREEDOM WHICH I RECEIVED.
THIS IS BUT A SMALL TOKEN OF MY APPRECIATION FOR YOUR EFFORTS
TO BRING ME COMFORT. I SHALL ALWAYS REMEMBER YOUR KINDNESS
AND GENEROSITY AS DO THE COUNTLESS SURVIVORS YOU HELPED FIFTY
YEARS AGO.

MARGIT FELDMAN
JULY, 1995

Replica of the plaque that Margit presented to the Judiska Museeti
(Jewish Museum) in Stockholm in 1995 to thank Sweden for that
country's role in her recovery following the Holocaust.

Margit meeting with Swedish librarians in Stockholm.

Margit with Hermina ("Minnie") Boehm, the aunt who became her second mother when she came to America.

Margit (left) with two Tolcsva friends, Cilika Green and Kati Roth, during a visit to Cleveland, Ohio.

Tombstone of Margit's mother and father at Yad Va Shem.

Tombstone, in Hungary, of Margit's uncle Henrik Buchhalter, the only other member of her European family who survived the Holocaust, and his two daughters, who died in Auschwitz.

The Holocaust Torah that Margit presented to her U.S. synagogue in 1986. The cover was designed by a fellow survivor.

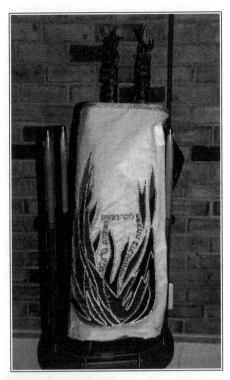

The crowns of the Holocaust Torah, crafted by Stanley Miller. The crowns resemble the barbed wire fences surrounding the death camps, from which bodies and arms reach to the skies.

Margit's school in Tolcsva, photographed during her 1996 visit.

Margit (left) in 1996 with residents of the home built on the land in Tolcsva where her house had once stood.

Margit (center) in Tolcsva in 1996 with two women she had known as a child.

Margit (back row, left of center) in 2002 with schoolchildren after a presentation on the Holocaust.

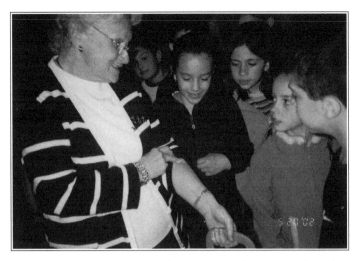

Margit in 2002, showing students the number tattooed on her arm.

Margit's family in 2000: left to right, son Joseph, daughter-in-law Julie holding Zachary, daughter Tina, Tina's daughter Caryn, Joseph's son Joshua, Margit, and Margit's husband, Harvey.

# 7

# From Hell to Recovery

Though we knew little of the developments as they occurred, the war was coming to an end. A few months after the beginning of our second stay in Auschwitz, in the early winter of 1944–45, my Aunt Elizabeth, Sari, and I became part of a group selected to be taken to Eastern Germany, to a subcamp of Gross Rosen, a place called Grunberg. Grunberg was one of many such subcamps of Gross Rosen, a huge complex dedicated largely to the production of armaments. At first we did not know the purpose of the selection. We were simply rushed into showers, disinfected, and given clean clothes for what was to be our journey into Germany.

Two thousand Polish and two thousand Hungarian women were sent to Grunberg from Auschwitz. There was already snow on the ground. As the war was coming to an end, the Germans, realizing that defeat was imminent, desperately sought slave laborers to work in the ammunition factory. The factory workers were primarily Hungarian. At least life in Grunberg was considerably better than that in Auschwitz. There was less harassment, cruelty, or brutality; we were less frequently beaten. One distinct advantage to Grunberg was that the food was more edible and the portions were larger than anything we had experienced before. It was to the Germans' advantage to keep us strong so that we could produce more bullets for the *Wehrmacht* (German army).

Every day we got up before dawn and went through the interminable roll call. After our morning meal, we were marched to the factory in rows of five, and were beaten if we got out of line. In the factory we sat at tables, each one of us mechanically and rapidly functioning as part of the process of transforming lead into bullets. If we slacked off, we were beaten or slapped. The punishment came not from the foreman, although he was German, but from the S.S. guards who were always nearby. I was slapped several times for being "too slow" or "too clumsy." The Germans were deathly afraid of sabotage.

There were residents of Grunberg who worked in the factory, too. They were, of course, paid employees who had privileges and benefits we lacked and were, for the most part, indifferent to our plight. They did not have the menial task of cleaning the work areas as we did. In fact, we had to clean their areas as well as ours! However, there were atypical incidents of cooperation on their part, particularly when we were in the bathroom; one or another of the German workers, usually an overseer, might secretly follow us in and pass to one of us an extra piece of bread they had hidden underneath their clothing. If we were lucky enough to experience this act of kindness, we had to eat the bread immediately lest the S.S. guards see us consume it and inflict punishment on both the giver and the receiver.

The Russians, enemies of the Germans, were now approaching us even more rapidly than before. We could tell that from the fact that the Grunberg S.S., both men and women, seemed uneasy. Soon they were ordered to move us again, but this time no transportation of any kind was supplied. We had to go on foot. My aunt and her sister-in-law were, of course, still with me. Although none of us knew it at the time, the Polish women were being marched in one direction, toward the Czechoslovak border, and the Hungarian women in another, toward Bergen-Belsen.

It was the dead of winter. We had no boots or winter clothes to protect us from the elements. The roads had not been cleared of snow from the constant snowfalls, so we were mired in the snow practically up to our waists and could barely put one foot before the other. For us it was literally a death march. There was no way in which we could keep up with the barking orders of the Germans, and those who collapsed under the weight of the struggle fell by the wayside and were left to freeze to death in the snow. Others who could not go on were shot to death. We had plenty of water, because we drank the melted snow. However, we had no food. On a few rare occasions we came across property on which there were farms, and we were allowed to spend the night in a barn, while the soldiers went into the farmers' houses. I could not understand at the time why they left us unguarded at night while they enjoyed the farmers' hospitality. But I realize now that they assumed we would perish from frost or starvation, fatigue or illness.

Since I had spent my growing-up years on a farm, I knew where to look for food. At home we had had no refrigerator or freezer where food could be stored, and I remembered how in the wintertime we would store vegetables underneath a cover of hay in order to keep them from freezing. So I rummaged busily to find what we could devour: beets, rutabaga, kohlrabi, and potatoes, whatever came into our hands. I would always find something, and we would eat it there in the barn. In one of the places we even found some live chickens. We grabbed the chickens, twisted their necks, plucked their feathers, ripped them apart, and ate them raw. Most of us got very sick as a result.

In our hunger, especially after the experience of Grunberg, where we had been comparatively "well fed," we found ourselves reduced to a primal state. Our starvation forced upon us an abandonment and a desperation most of us had not known before. Food was almost the only element of life that mattered. Yet despite our condition, we tried as much as we could to share what we had, and never, even in the horror of those last desperate days, did we resort to a consideration of cannibalism. I know that there are people who claim that some survivors indulged in the eating of human flesh, but never, never in my experience did I encounter its presence in thought, word, or deed.

Among the Polish women in Grunberg had been a young girl named Gerda Weissman. I had not met her in the camp. She was among those sent to the Czech border. In 1989 I attended a United Jewish Appeal fundraiser in my community of Bridgewater, New Jersey. The key speaker at this fundraiser was a survivor by the name of Gerda Weissman Klein, a writer who had penned *All But My Life*, her autobiography of her years in the Holocaust and after. While she was speaking, I listened as though in a stupor. I realized that we had been in Grunberg together.

After the program I approached her, introducing myself as a fellow survivor from Grunberg, and we embraced and shed tears. The audience was bewildered at what they saw, and we had to explain to them the reason for our emotional state. All these people, whom I knew so well myself, began to cry.

At another time, following this presentation, Gerda spoke at the annual Holocaust and Genocide Seminar at Raritan Valley College in Branchburg, New Jersey. Once she spoke by herself and once with her husband, Kurt Klein. Kurt had been a lieutenant in the American army that had liberated the area of

Silesia, where Gerda was at the end of the war. He had been a young German Jew but had been able to emigrate from Germany before World War II. He had desperately tried to get his parents out of Germany, but had been tragically unsuccessful. He and Gerda fell in love after he had discovered her, and they married.

After marching for countless days, we arrived at our final destination: Bergen-Belsen. No words can convey accurately or graphically enough the horrors of that place. As we entered the camp, we saw piles and piles of bodies rotting away. The biting winter cold was still around us, and the bodies were already frozen. Nevertheless, this did not retard the decaying process. We had never before seen so vividly the results of mass murder, and it shocked us that these corpses were not accorded the dignity of burial, even in a mass grave.

I can close my eyes today and visualize everything as it was when I entered the camp for the first time. We were all weakened, hungry, and sick from our long ordeal on the death march. We surely did not expect to find a God-forsaken, death-filled hell such as this at its end. In virtually no time at all, though, we absorbed and became part of this environment.

Inside the camp the inmates were suffering from typhus, dysentery, and diphtheria; their bodies were covered with lice. The entire group of women with whom I had arrived were suffering from lice less than twenty-four hours after arriving at Bergen-Belsen. The lice began to attack with a vengeance the moment we arrived, and ate away at us continually. No sooner had we removed them then they came back over our bodies.

There were no sanitation or medical facilities. My Aunt Elizabeth, Sari, and I all contracted typhus and diphtheria. We were soon in such a weakened condition that we hadn't even the strength to go outside when we were allowed to in order to relieve ourselves. We lay literally caked with excrement, which we could smell on our own bodies and on those of others. But there was nothing we could do, so debilitated and feeble were we. As we observed the death and dying around us, we finally lost our will to live, feeling that we had been abandoned by the world.

Sari was the first to die. She was small and not very strong. She lasted no longer than a week. Then my aunt went, probably no more than a few days before liberation. Aunt Elizabeth had been a beautiful and vibrant woman, and she had lasted through all of the earlier horrors. In those terrible days, she had been my link to my past life and my family. She had been my constant companion through the nightmares of Auschwitz, Cracow, Grunberg, and the death march." Now, at what was to be the terminus of my ordeal, I was alone. My only connection to the world of my past was some fellow survivors from Hungary, who still managed to cling to life.

Whatever "nourishment" we received from the rotting potatoes we found strewn about the camp was so sparse and so miserable that the strongest among us could not be sustained by it. I watched my rabbi's wife die, along with her younger daughter. Hundreds died daily. Those of us who managed to evade death and were physically able to do so would take the bodies and put them outside the bunker so we would not have to sleep next to them. In the process we took some of their clothing and their shoes. We didn't think about the "rightness" or "wrongness" of what we did. All that mattered to us was survival—not our mere physical survival, but survival for the sake of showing the world what the Nazis and their surrogates had done to us, when all the while the world had remained silent and indifferent.

On Sunday, April 15, 1945, at about 3 p.m., liberation came. It arrived almost by accident when the Eleventh Armored Division of the Second British Army came across the camp in their push through northwest Germany. My personal recollections of that episode are almost entirely bottled up in my memory and simply refuse to open themselves to expression. I remember a commotion, a great deal of yelling in English, and even some Yiddish, especially the words "*Frei! Frei!*" There were men in uniforms, but only some wore German uniforms. The rest, we learned, were British.

The British soldiers were handing out chocolate and other delicacies and trying to get people to talk. They were attempting to pull us out of our barracks, which were infested with bugs, germs, and lice. They were trying to pull those who were still alive and mobile away from those who were already dead or near death. All the while the British were trying to penetrate our consciousness with words like "Free. Free. Don't you know you are free?"

Once the British soldiers had pulled us out of our barracks, they began working on us to rid us of all the filth and infestations our bodies had acquired during those days in Belsen, and even before. I can recall that we were sitting outside the barracks as the area around us was being hosed down. As the water came streaming out of the hoses, those inmates who were strong enough ran through the streams, trying to scrub their bodies and their hair and get some water in their mouths. I remained in a sitting position, and when the water hit me I was able to wash myself. The soldiers were able to clean us off, but the barracks were another matter. There was no way they could get the bugs and germs and disease out of those. They had to use flame-throwers to burn the barracks down.

I recall now how, after the soldiers pulled me from that God-forsaken barrack, I wanted only to crawl on my hands and knees to the corpses stacked so high and start looking for my beloved mother and father. I must have snapped for a while, but then I realized that I was being pulled away from the corpses by other survivors who were huddling close to each other, crying and praying, "God, help us!"

Fewer than twenty-four hours after liberation began, units of the Royal Army Medical Corps arrived, evacuated the camp, and established a hospital within what had very recently been the German Army barracks. Typhus control was also begun. It was necessary to bury the dead.

By this time all the German S.S. who had been trying to escape had been rounded up. The British general, Brigadier General H. L. Glyn Hughes, made those in German uniforms do the same dirty work the British soldiers had until now been forced to do. He wanted the Germans to see what they and their leaders had done to us. The Germans were made to clean up the camp. They were also compelled to dig graves and to bury the rotting corpses. Many of these "strong," "heroic," and "dedicated" Germans found the task too much for them, so a bulldozer was requisitioned to push countless anonymous, unrecognizable bodies into mass graves. The chaplains and rabbis of the British Army conducted services.

To this day I remain amazed and appalled that the horrors of Bergen-Belsen could have existed in the vicinity of the pleasant towns and cities of the Rhineland, and that no one would have been shamed or shocked by the deeds of their compatriots—or even aware of them! Just a few days after liberation several *Burgermeisters* (mayors) of neighboring areas and a number of *Wehrmacht* officers were taken around the camp to be shown the horror that had existed in their midst. Of those who were forced to view the remnants of horror and suffering, only one or two showed any degree of indignation or revulsion. Most simply shrugged to indicate that they had not known. Surely one cannot deny that the press had been held captive by the Nazi regime, but for these otherwise benign and civilized people not to know what was going on under their very noses was inconceivable.

Those of us with sufficient strength were allowed to go into town to ask if we could take some food. A few of my friends from the camp went in and brought back some packs of beef, vegetables, and potatoes in order to try to cook a stew. The candy bars and other foods that the soldiers had distributed to us were too rich for most of our systems; many prisoners contracted terrible diarrhea and stomach disorders that, in several instances, proved fatal. There was a terrible and poignant irony in the fact that so many prisoners, after suffering from malnutrition and starvation, should now die from overconsumption. But such was our situation. Some of us realized we could digest only the simplest of foods.

We got some twigs, made a small fire, and put a pot on it. Suddenly there was an explosion. The cause of the explosion was some live ammunition buried under our fire that the Germans had planted before escaping. They had wanted to cover up the evidence of what had happened in Bergen-Belsen, but didn't get to finish the job before the British arrived. They had also attempted to sabotage the water supply. They wanted to make certain that we did not enjoy the freedom we had finally found.

I had been sitting near the explosion, and ended up with a piece of shrapnel on the left side of my head, underneath the skin. Fortunately, it didn't penetrate anything vital; however, I can feel it to this day. I also had a piece of shrapnel under my left arm near my breast. My left thigh had a large hole in it. I called my wounds Hitler's footsteps on my body.

I was taken by the Red Cross into the army hospital, and thereby lost my new-found freedom. I was sick; I cannot even say how sick. I came down with pleurisy and pneumonia. I remember that I was burning up with a fever, but I got very skilled and caring treatment from the Red Cross.

I felt great desolation in the hospital. The wounds on my body could be cleaned and bandaged, but not the wounds on my psyche. I was all alone, filled with sadness and bewilderment, loneliness and terror. I was fifteen years old. I did not know the whereabouts or fates of my family; I did not know where I would go or what I would do. I had been brought up to have a deep sense of spirituality and a strong belief in God. Eventually I began to pray every day that one day soon my mother and father would walk into the hospital room where I was staying and whisk me away to our home, where our normal life would resume. But they never came. Nothing happened, yet I began to feel less alone, so the prayers must have done some good.

When I recollect my time in Bergen-Belsen, I think of Anne Frank, whose birthday I shared. I truly sensed that we were connected to one another. She, too, was an inmate of the camp, but she did not survive. She died of typhus before she could experience the sense of knowing again what it meant to be free. We were exactly the same age. I will always feel that our fates could have easily been interchanged.

While I was in the hospital, an extraordinary thing happened. One day a young woman walked through the doors of our hospital ward. Speaking in a gentle and cultured voice, she informed us that there were ships waiting to take us to Sweden. This woman, we were told, was a member of the Swedish royal family, and I had to rub my eyes to make certain I was not dreaming. Her name was Princess Bernadotte. Was this some kind of fairy tale? Was it a dream in which one's hopes and fantasies would be fulfilled?

Sweden had had a checkered history vis-à-vis the Jews. Jews were not permitted in Sweden until the eighteenth century. The influence of Luther's anti-Semitism was very strong before and during that period of Swedish history. The first Jew to enter the country was a renowned Jewish physician named Benedictus de Castro, who was called in to treat Queen Christina in 1673. For a long time after the first Jews were allowed into the country, they were governed by severe limitations as to where they might live, whom they might marry, and to what professions they might belong. In the mid–nineteenth century, there was a gradual loosening of restrictions that culminated in the establishment of full civil rights for Swedish Jews in 1870. Jews gradually began to be assimilated into Swedish society. They inhabited, and continue to inhabit, large cities like Stockholm, Malmo, and Gothenberg.

Sweden's sheltering of Jewish refugees from Germany had begun in the 1930s, although under very limited conditions. For most of the Hitler years and World War II, Sweden had maintained the same neutrality it had practiced since the nineteenth century, but now the nations surrounding Sweden were under Nazi occupation and were less inclined to help in the way they had during the refugee crises in the 1930s. In 1938 Jewish refugees trying to enter Sweden were sent back to their home countries, and were thereby doomed to death. During World War II, Swedish "neutrality" had begun to crumble, and sympathy had tilted toward the Germans.

However, in the fall of 1943, when the Jews of Denmark were about to be deported, Sweden was called upon to give asylum to some eight thousand Danish Jews, and it accepted that responsibility.

In June of 1944, King Gustav V of Sweden sent a letter of protest to Hungary's regent, Admiral Horthy, regarding the persecution and deportation of Hungarian Jewry in the spring of that year. This letter, as well as pressure from the Allied governments, ended the Hungarian deportations early in the summer of 1944, weeks after my family and I had been removed from our village. At the same time, Raoul Wallenberg, an attaché to the Swedish legation in Budapest, was helping to rescue thousands of Hungarian Jews from the Arrow Cross, the Hungarian Fascist Party. The Swedes also rescued several hundred Danish Jews imprisoned in Theresienstadt. At the very end of the war, even Heinrich Himmler, the head of the German Security Police, met with leaders of the World Jewish Congress and Count Folke Bernadotte of the Swedish Red Cross to discuss the release of Jews from German concentration camps. In the weeks following the end of the war, thousands of Jews were taken to Sweden for physical and mental rehabilitation. I was one of those Jews.

I remember the journey from Germany to Sweden. Aboard ship many of the passengers, including myself, were suffering from pleurisy. I could not breathe; my lungs were filled with water. I was suffering both from the water in my lungs and from the wounds incurred during the explosion. But I sensed that God was watching over me, and that the Swedish people who transported us were our "guardian angels." Upon our arrival in Sweden, we landed in Malmo. Ambulances were waiting to take those of us to who direly needed medical attention to Carlstad, where there was a hospital. None of us could really understand Swedish, but we knew the people were helping us.

When we arrived in Carlstad, we were put in a hospital setting, in a large ward. I discovered that I was suffering from dysentery, typhus, diphtheria, and loss of hair. Like so many others, I was cleaned and cared for. Nurses put their arms around me and calmed me down. For the first time in over a year, I felt what it meant to be hugged and comforted, to have someone reassure me with words and gestures. Whatever fear or trepidation I might have experienced, even after the liberation and the journey to Sweden, was now being washed away in the tide of affection and caring that now swept over me.

Some time went by. I am not even certain how many weeks. People came from within the city of Carlstad and from other parts of Sweden. They brought us food, clothing, and other items we needed and even "luxury" items that made us believe we were human again. It felt to me as though Heaven were opening, and the certainty that there was still goodness in the world overwhelmed me. It also restored me to sanity. In the hospital I was interviewed by someone from HIAS (the Hebrew Sheltering and Immigration Society), the organization that worked with Jewish immigrants, helping them to cope with new surroundings and the adjustments made in their lives, and also helping them to find out what might have happened to members of their families. It was there and then that I found out what I had most dreaded to know: that my parents and nearly all the other members of my family had perished, with the exception of my uncle Henrik, who had survived and returned to Hungary. In that shattering moment of revelation, all hope of return to the familiarity and normalcy of my childhood world vanished.

To me, it was unthinkable that I would ever return to Hungary to live. So I was virtually alone. The sorrow that I felt at my loss of family and other close connections was at least accompanied by a sense of closure. Until that time I had known nothing and could only speculate about the fates of those dear to me. I could only continue to hope, against all signs to the contrary, that I would be reunited with them. But I was also experiencing a terrible enlightenment. One ought never to experience at the age of sixteen, my age by then, the sadness and bewilderment of being alone in the world.

The first six months of my stay in Sweden was spent in the hospital in Carlstad. With the help of the caring Swedish doctors and nurses and the kind citizens of the community, I gradually regained my health and became a "normal human being" all over again. The people who visited me every day—total strangers—brought clothing and food, but mostly they brought welcome hugs and kisses. There was no real verbal communication because of the language barrier, but I did not need it. I could feel the love that came from those people. To this day I call them my guardian angels.

It was during this time that I began to think and rethink my past. All that had been precious to me—my mother, my father, my grandmother, and my home—had been lost to me. I was not alone in this loss. Like thousands of others, I had been wrenched from familiar surroundings, from the love of family, from preparations for a bright future, by a bestial wave of terror. I was now haunted by memories of lost traditions of the Sabbath and festivals, of the varied seasons, of the animals with which I had played as "friends," of joyous family reunions and the comfort of the known. I had dreadful flashbacks of familiar surroundings suddenly becoming alien and sinister, of neighbors becoming strangers. No rescue came from the liberating armies, from the democratic nations warring against Hitler. The question "Where was the free world?" echoed and reechoed like a persistent drumming in my head.

When I was again ambulatory, I was given twelve-hour passes to see what "normal" life was like. On days like these, townspeople used to come to the hospital and pick me up and take me to their homes for the day. I was seldom without the help, guidance, and encouragement of one or another of these fine Swedish people.

When I was finally discharged from the hospital, I was given a factory job, along with several other survivors. We spent our time together not only at work, but during leisure periods as well. We lived not in overcrowded displaced persons camps, as many other survivors did, but in individual cottages, where we enjoyed both the privacy of living on our own and the camaraderie of each other. It was my first "home" since leaving Tolcsva two years before.

Because the Swedish government was highly efficient and well organized, it was able to watch over me even after I was dismissed from the hospital. Although the wounds of war and the sense of personal bereavement were still with me, I felt at home in that wonderful country. I even learned the Swedish language well enough that I could understand it when I went on a visit to Sweden two years ago. I was certainly not alone in my affection for the country and its people: approximately one-third of my group of survivors elected to remain in Sweden and to become Swedish citizens.

There were not only Hungarian Jews in Sweden. There were Greek Jews, Italian Jews, and Jews of many other nationalities in this country, where they had found a haven. For the first time I truly had a sense of the breadth and depth of experience of other European Jews during those terrible days.

I never expected to return to Hungary, especially after I found out that all of my family had been killed. I was planning to make *Aliyah* to Israel, which meant to become an inhabitant of the Jewish land (which was yet to be formed, but whose formation was being discussed) and to give it my full loyalty.

I was already booked on a boat when I received a telegram from my aunts and uncles in New York. An uncle on my mother's side, George, who lived in Brooklyn, had spotted an advertisement placed by HIAS in the Hungarian-American newspaper, with my name listed as one of those seeking relatives in the United States. He informed my aunt, my father's sister Hermina ("Minnie") Buchhalter Boehm, of that fact. Just before my Aunt Elizabeth had died she had told me that if I survived and everyone else perished, I should look for my Aunt Minnie, her older sister, and she would care for me as a mother. She passed away in February 2000. I used to visit her as often as I could, and when I was with her I seemed able, by simply looking into her face, to recreate my father and the lost members of his family.

My Aunt Minnie, my Uncle Fred (her husband), and their daughter Clara had been going regularly to HIAS headquarters to find out if any names of family members were listed as survivors. While there one day, they encountered Uncle George, who was also seeking family survivors. He carried a newspaper written in Hungarian to which he pointed and said, "Our niece is looking for us." My Aunt Minnie tells me that at that moment, they all realized they were all connected by blood to the same person. They began to weep with joy and to embrace one another. There was at least one survivor from their families in Hungary!

Almost immediately my American relatives wrote to me, asking me to identify myself and my Hungarian family so that they would know I was truly their niece. Not for a moment did I hesitate. I knew then and there that the decision to respond to their letter would be my most profound decision and would begin my boldest journey.

On October 3, 1945, in response to their communication, I wrote the following letter to my Aunt Minnie in Hungarian (my Cousin Clara translated it from Hungarian to English):

Karlstad, October 3, 1945
Dear beloved Aunt Hermina and kind family,

I received your letter this very day, and it was with great happiness that I read it. I already sent you a telegram and another letter, which I hope you have already received. Thank God, I now feel much better. Your letter poured new strength and hope into me.

I will now write of other matters. On March 19, 1944, the Germans came into Hungary. That was the day when our lives were marked. We were then living in Tolcsva. Soon after that they gathered all the Jews together and took us to Ujhel, where we remained for six weeks in the ghetto. We were quartered together with Uncle Henrik, Aunt Elizabeth, and grandmother, in the ghetto. We went through countless hardships there. After that we all went to Auschwitz, and there we were sorted apart; men, women, and children were separated. There I was parted from my mother and father, and put together with Aunt Elizabeth and her husband's sister, Sara Grunhut. I don't even have to write of it, most certainly you must have heard how we starved, suffered, and were forced to work dreadfully hard. My dearly loved ones could not bear the work and starvation as I could.

They both died in my arms on April 27, 1945. Therefore, I am now left completely alone. I cannot write you anything at all about anyone else. I have written several times to the Consuls to inquire about my beloved ones. They took all the particulars and said they would make announcements over the radio, and thus try to find them if they live. After we were liberated from Bergen-Belsen, I was wounded by an explosion caused by a fire, which left me with four shrapnel wounds. I was laid up for six weeks, but I am now much better. We will discuss all this in person.

You ask whether I want to come to you. What would I go home for? I haven't anyone at all to go back to. I couldn't exist alone anyway in this large world. I'm still young, and have the need of a mother's love and care, which you, Aunt Hermina, can supply. Beloved Aunt Elizabeth's dying words were, if in any way I survived I should contact you at my first opportunity, because you would be a second mother to me.

I'm writing this letter, but I'm crying so, that it is very difficult for me to continue. I can't possibly write down what heartaches I feel.

You asked about Uncle Henrik's two little girls. Edith was fourteen, and little Elizabeth was nine years old, when I last saw them a year and a half ago. Since then I know nothing of them. I'll give you my vital statistics. I, Margit Buchhalter, was born in Budapest, June 12, 1929. My last address was Tolcsva.

I can hardly wait for the moment when I can hug you in my arms Aunt Hermina. Clara, darling, I was able to read your handwriting very easily. I thank you from the bottom of my heart for your kind invitation.

I would love to see you all already, then we will talk over everything together. Your family picture came out very nicely. I sent you a picture of myself, but it is not very good. I will send you a better as soon as possible.

Clara, dear, you ask me what I need. I have no desires left at all. The Germans killed everything inside of me a year and a half ago. The Swedish people gave me one each of every article of clothing. Clara, you probably can imagine what I could use. Clara, dear, please send me my Uncle George's address. I would like to write to him also. I would love to be with you as soon as possible. Now I won't write more. I am together with a girl from my hometown.

With all my love and kisses to you all,

Your little sister,

Margit

Aunt Minnie Boehm, particularly, was so anxious for my arrival that she was willing to have her son, who was in the U.S. Army stationed in Europe, marry me and bring me here as a war bride. This proved to be unnecessary. There were also three brothers of my mother living here: Morris, Sam, and George. Sam's wife's sister, who was connected to HIAS, helped them to obtain affidavits attesting to the fact that I would not be a burden to the U.S. government. Finally, after several months of delay and anxiety, hope, and fear, in the summer of 1946 I was prepared to set sail for what would be my new home in the United States.

No one can fully understand the feelings of excitement and fright one experiences at moments like that. My fellow survivors who were with me in Carlstadt gave me a going-away party. We cried and made promises never to forget one another and what we had been through, and they all accompanied me to the place from which my boat was to depart. They stood there waving as the ship pulled out of the harbor. My emotions were terribly mixed: while I was both terrified and happy for myself, I was melancholy for those of my friends who still had no place to go and no one to go to.

# 8

# New Life in America

I traveled by boat across the ocean with many other refugees. We came across on a Swedish ship, the *Drotling Holm*. Ill as I was from seasickness during the voyage, I made the best of it. On the boat, people made friends with one another. There were many survivors among us. When the boat arrived finally in New York Harbor, an announcement came over the loudspeaker: "Margit Buchhalter, please come to the captain's quarters."

At that moment, I began to die inside. I said to myself, "Now they've discovered something wrong with me and they will send me back." I went through a lifetime of inner torture in the few minutes of that interminable walk to the captain's quarters. As I entered (and this is a scene I will never forget), I was amazed to discover my aunt, a man I took to be my Uncle George, and my Uncle Sam's sister-in-law, who had helped to make the arrangements to meet me and to welcome me into the country. They had gotten permission to come onto the boat in order to take me off of it. How did I know immediately that one of the women was my aunt, my father's sister? She had a face nearly identical to that of my father! For a moment I had truly thought I was looking into my father's face!

All at once I fell completely apart. I had traveled thousands of miles, and I saw someone who looked like my father standing before me. It took me a few minutes to compose myself and to resume speaking rationally.

Because my family took me off the boat, I never had to go through the endless immigration processing of Ellis Island— the continual checking, cross-checking, and questioning that others had to go through. We were taken by tugboat into the landing area. I know of no other fellow survivors who were received by the United States and their families in such a remarkable way. There were cars waiting for us when we got off the tugboat. The rest of the family was there—aunts, uncles, cousins. These were members of both sides of my family. We drove to the Bronx, where my Aunt Minnie lived at 2147 Starling Avenue, and we had a joyous reunion. I felt that I was floating on air. I could not believe that all of this could be real: family, food on the table, warmth, and joy. Instinctively I began peering at the faces of the group, looking for my father and mother. But they weren't there. I discovered later that this was a "normal" reaction.

My Uncle Fred, Minnie's husband, who had stayed at home while the others came to the boat, was the maître d' at a Hungarian restaurant in New York. While they were gone he and his two daughters, Clara and Miriam, had set a table fit for royalty. I had not seen food like that for over two years, since I had been taken from my home. The aroma was so pungent and inviting that I can still close my eyes and smell (and even taste) that food, though that was over fifty years ago. This display of family unity and love helped me to regain the sense of security I had not known since my departure from Tolcsva.

At this gathering were aunts and uncles, their children and grandchildren, and my father's first cousins, the Weiss family (the children of my paternal grandmother's twin sister). I had never met any of the people who now surrounded me, but their faces bore family resemblances to those of my mother, father, and grandparents. The Weisses gave me the best of all possible gifts: the independence of a savings account in my own name. They had deposited into it $500, which was a great deal of money at that time, so that I could purchase necessities and be independent and self-sufficient.

Communication between us was difficult. The only ones who spoke Hungarian were Aunt Minnie, Uncle Fred, and their daughters, Clara and Miriam. My mother's brothers and George's wife also spoke Hungarian. Their sons Philip and Willie understood the language, but did not speak it very well. The others, however, communicated with love in their eyes and smiles on their faces and with hugs and kisses. These wordless gestures proved to be medicine for my soul, which no doctor could have ever prescribed.

Amid the joy of being with my newfound family was another satisfaction: the realization that Hitler had not completely succeeded. A remnant of us was still here!

I continued living in the Bronx with my Aunt Minnie and visited my uncles and their families in Brooklyn on weekends. I realized immediately that I had to learn the English language. Since it was August, Aunt Minnie was anxious to enroll me in some form of school where I could begin to learn English and resume my education. She was able to register me in James Monroe High School, but my time as a pupil there was short-lived since my English was so poor at the time. Then my family found a school near the Hunts Point area of the Bronx. This school was strictly for new immigrants, and it was there that I learned enough reading, writing, and spelling of English to qualify as a worker and to enable me to get through everyday life in the United States.

To my sorrow, my Uncle Fred passed away within a year of my arrival in the United States. Since he worked nights, he would sleep during the day and was available on school days to meet my bus in the afternoon. I remember how he would greet me with a hug and a kiss and a delicious ice cream cone. He had become to me a father figure whom I had come to love and greatly respect. His sudden passing was another blow I had to sustain, and it opened the wounds of my recent life all over again.

Early one morning he had come home from work and gone to bed. Suddenly we heard a terrible gasping noise, and I heard my aunt scream. Their two sons and I ran into the bedroom, where we found him prostrate and gasping for air; then we ran to get his daughters Miriam, who lived on the same floor of the apartment building where we lived, and Clara, who lived in the next building. By the time the girls and the ambulance had arrived, he was already dead. For a long time I felt inconsolable.

In the meantime I developed sisterlike relationships with both Clara and Miriam. This boosted my morale, and made my losses more bearable than they might have been. Miriam and Clara were only a few years older than I. Both were in their twenties and married, but it didn't matter; we were like contemporaries. They and their husbands showed me New York and helped me to become acclimated to America.

Miriam had two boys, Morton and Stanley. When they were little, Morton, who was about seven when I arrived in this country, used to try to teach me English by spelling out words for me. He thought that by spelling out the words he would be able to make me understand them. Unfortunately, this did not work.

I often visited my mother's brothers, Morris, George, and Sam, who lived in Coney Island. I would stay at George's house with him and Eleanor, his wife. They lived upstairs, and their son Stanley and his wife Ruth, with whom I still have very close relationships, lived downstairs. His other son, Alfred, did not live in the same area, so I did not see him often.

On the occasion of these visits, we spent time talking about Tolcsva and our lives there. George remembered it because he had returned to Tolscva in 1927 to visit his parents. I had not yet been born at the time, but we had many memories to share of our family and the town. When I visited them in Coney Island, I remember taking long, pleasurable walks with George on the boardwalk. We also spent time on the beach. I loved the nearness of the ocean, and this love has stayed with me to this day.

Two blocks away from George and his family lived my Uncle Morris and his wife, Minnie. I was particularly close to their children, Louis, Jerry, and Rose. I remember on summer days enjoying ice cream cones with them and chatting on the front steps of the family house. Louis and Jerry had both been in the war, and they told me of their experiences and memories. Jerry had been in the Air Force and described the awesome experience of flying over enemy territory. He still has his bomber jacket, which he said he would never get rid of. Rose was married to Arthur, who still spoke Hungarian although he had been born here. He had a mischievous sense of humor, and told me jokes and stories in Hungarian that always made me laugh and bewildered my other cousins, who couldn't understand what we were saying. Arthur was able to bring lightness to my mood when I became despondent.

My Uncle Sam and his wife, Stella, also lived in Brooklyn, but to visit them I had to make a separate trip. My Aunt Stella's sister was the one who had helped get me to America. I developed a very warm relationship with their son Seymour and his wife, Helen. Sam had a daughter, too, from his first marriage, but I have not been able to recall her name.

Those of my cousins from my mother's side with whom I am still very close and with whom I still socialize are Rose, Jerry and his wife, Marion, as well as Stanley's wife, Ruth, Seymour's wife, Helen, and Alfred's wife, Stella. We still visit each other and continually strengthen the bond among us each year when we spend our winters in Florida.

On my father's side, Aunt Minnie's son Willie and his wife, Vera, are still alive. So are my Cousin Philip's wife, Harriet, and Gail and Sari Ellen, their children. Willie and Vera have three children, Fred, Linda, and Larry. Willie was like the brother I never had. When I first met him, he was still in his army uniform. He was always there to help me with my school-work, and at times he drove me to Brooklyn to visit other members of my family so that I did not have to go alone. We are still in very close contact. We speak by telephone at least twice a week. Philip was about ten years older. He had a car with a rumble seat where I used to sit. He would drive me around Manhattan, and I loved to gape at the sights, never having imagined earlier that I would see Times Square, the Empire State Building, or Rockefeller Center. Philip also introduced me to the American hot dog. We could not pass a kosher delicatessen without stopping and buying one, and hot dogs became an addiction for me. On certain evenings Philip would drive my aunt and me to the Hungarian section of the city, in the East Seventies, where we would stop at coffee houses for iced coffee and *dobbosh tortes*, wonderful Hungarian pastries. On other evenings he would take me to the movies, because he thought the experience of watching American movies would teach me English. He would explain words and their meanings, much to the annoyance of the other theater patrons.

Philip passed away on November 15, 1987, the very day that my granddaughter Caryn was born, thus darkening an otherwise joyous event.

After Uncle Fred died, I stopped my schooling and found a job with Spear's Furniture Company on West Twenty-third Street. There I worked as a filing clerk. It was the easiest job for me to obtain, since the alphabet is the same in Hungarian as in English. I took the subway down from the Bronx every morning. At Spear's the people were friendly and helpful to me, and I felt comfortable with them despite the language barrier. There was a dark-haired Jewish girl there who helped me to socialize, to dress more attractively, and even to flirt. I also met a young man named Arnold with whom I began to keep company.

Just at the time I felt my life beginning to bloom, as any young adult's might, I became ill. It was May 1948; I was not yet nineteen. During a very short stay at Bronx Hospital I was diagnosed as having tuberculosis. With the help of my cousin Jack Weiss, I could be admitted to Brooklyn Thoracic Hospital. Over a month's time I had many tests. I took a great deal of medication, which made me ill. While I was there I celebrated my nineteenth birthday. A Doctor Rudolphe took care of me at the hospital. My own doctor was named Lou Green, and he is a brother to Adolph Green, the actor and writer. They were my father's second cousins. Dr. Green was the one who had referred me to Bronx Hospital.

While I was at Brooklyn Thoracic, I met several patients with whom I made friends, and my American family visited me daily. While I was there one of my cousins, Julius, married, and my family sent the bridal bouquet to the hospital. I met a young man named Murray Dennet, who was a patient there also, and we kept company for a while afterward. While we were in the hospital, he wrote me letters from his room. My roommate Rose teased me about him.

I remained at Brooklyn Thoracic from May 14 until early December. On December 7, 1948, I was transferred from Brooklyn Thoracic to Bedford Hills Sanitarium, where my cousins Clara and Jack Weiss took me. Being there was very frightening and depressing. The physical distance between my family and me was now greater than ever. They were able to visit me only on weekends. Many tests were done on me, including a bronchoscopy.

In the spring of 1950, as I was approaching my twenty-first birthday, the decision was made to transfer me to Montefiore Hospital in the Bronx. The doctors thought I should have surgery. My Aunt Minnie and Clara and two of my mother's brothers, George and Sam, came to confer with me and with the doctors at Montefiore. After listening to the description of the procedure and the danger of the surgery given them by a surgeon, Dr. Rubin, my uncles felt that I should not attempt major surgery for fear of the outcome and the repercussions, which could have left me crippled for life. They felt it would be better for me to remain in the sanitarium for the rest of my life. Whether they felt this way out of fear or out of love I do not know to this day. However, I did not question their opinion.

Aunt Minnie and Cousin Clara did not agree. How could I, they argued, a young woman not yet twenty-one, give up the possibility of a normal married life, with the hope of having children, and abandon everything to a life in the sanitarium? In retrospect, I realize that they were absolutely right. I also had a talk with Dr. Rubin. He felt that because of my youth and energy I could survive the surgery and have a full and normal life.

The decision had to be my own. I opted for surgery. The doctors performed a three-stage thoracoplasty on my right lung.

My right lung was collapsed, and seven ribs were removed on my right side. For each of three months I underwent a stage of the procedure, and as a result, I was later able to meet and marry my husband, Harvey, and bear two wonderful children, Tina and Joseph.

Each time I came out of the operating room after a stage of the procedure, my Aunt Minnie and Clara were at my bedside for hours and hours. I remember Aunt Minnie wiping my forehead with cold water. She would bring homemade meals to Montefiore every day. With her care and her loving encouragement, she became the single most significant reason for my regaining my strength. My uncles were, of course, happy in retrospect, even though they had originally discouraged me from taking the steps I did.

After I became ambulatory again, I was walking around the veranda one day, and a young man called to me from his room to invite me in. He had been hospitalized for tuberculosis, too. We met and talked, and I found out that, to use his words, he "could go for" me, a bit of English vernacular I was already able to understand. But our conversation at that time did not lead me to believe that anything would develop from it.

In the fall of 1950 I was transferred back to Bedford Hills. A van there took us for recuperation activities. One day when the van returned to the front entrance, the same young man I had seen at Montefiore was standing at a second-floor window looking down. He saw me, though I didn't see him. Later he told me he had decided then and there that I was the girl he was going to marry. I had had an understanding all along with Murray Dennet that there was a serious relationship between him and me, but as soon as Harvey Feldman, the young man at the window, made known his serious feelings for me, I realized that he was my choice for a husband. There was an instant chemistry between us.

Our relationship began to flourish then and there. We went to movies together. We sat together in the dining room. Harvey introduced me to his parents. I felt that we were very good for one another, and I was hoping that he felt the same way.

Once I recuperated enough to begin to think of a vocation for myself, I began to study X-ray technology at Bedford Hills. I eventually became a technician and worked in the X-ray department, and I continued to see Harvey. He gradually recovered from tuberculosis, which he had contracted while in the National Guard, and left Bedford Hills. I had convinced him to go into some aspect of the medical field. He went to the Eastern School for Physician Aides, where he became a medical technologist.

On weekends Harvey came up to visit me at Bedford Hills or I went to the Bronx to stay with my aunt and he came there to visit me. I cooked delicious meals for him. Our courtship continued. We wrote and talked to one another even when he couldn't see me. When he went to Bedford Hills, the bucolic surroundings became an ideal place for our courtship.

While we were keeping company, Harvey asked me why I had decided to stay in Bedford Hills and not return to live in the Bronx. The fact was—and I had learned this from my cousin Clara—that once I had contracted tuberculosis, Aunt Minnie felt reluctant to have me live in her apartment, considering that her two sons still lived with her and she didn't want them or the rest of her family exposed to a communicable disease. She had had a sister, Ethel, who had married a man with tuberculosis who had never told her of the fact. Ethel had contracted the disease from her husband and died of it. Much as I was saddened at not being able to live there, I realized that the dread of tuberculosis, which had already struck my father's family, had left an ineradicable scar on my aunt. My Aunt Minnie's decision never lessened my love for her, since she had been instrumental in helping me make my decision to live a normal life.

Once Harvey graduated from school, we began to make arrangements for our wedding. Harvey's first job was as an X-ray and laboratory technician at Bound Brook Hospital in Bound Brook, New Jersey. Since he had been brought up with the notion that a man does not marry until he can support his wife, we had gone together for four years.

In April 1953 he began working at Bound Brook Hospital. I went there for an interview in September 1953, just before Yom Kippur. I met Dr. Benjamin Borow, who shared with his brother Henry a medical practice located right next door to Bound Brook Hospital. He hired me right on the spot, then took me home to meet his wife, Beatrice. Beatrice took one look at me and said, with Harvey standing there, "If I had a single son, you would have become my daughter and part of my family." From that day on I *became* a part of her family. Even today, I remain very close to her two sons and their wives, Edward Borow and Rosalie and Maxwell Borow and Eleanor, his first wife, and Carolyn, his present wife, and all their children.

Dr. Borow dispensed medications to his patients, and I assisted him.

I got the job in September and gave two weeks' notice to my employers at Bedford Hills. I moved to New Jersey and lived in a room in the upstairs attic of Bound Brook Hospital, where other employees, including Harvey, also lived. I was beginning a whole new phase of my life.

Harvey and I were married on December 13, 1953. Our wedding took place at Moskowitz and Lupowitz Restaurant, a kosher

Hungarian-Jewish establishment on the Lower East Side of Manhattan. A rabbi performed the ceremony. Both of our families attended, as well as Dr. and Mrs. Benjamin Borow, Dr. and Mrs. Henry Borow, and Dr. and Mrs. Cutter. Dr. Cutter was a resident at Bound Brook Hospital. My one regret was that my mother and father were not there to walk me down the aisle in the wedding service. Nor were the others of my European relatives who had perished in the *Shoah*.

Our honeymoon was spent at the Nevele Country Club in the Catskills, and immediately afterward we returned to Bound Brook. We lived in a tiny attic apartment. The building we lived in belonged to Dr. Louis Borow, a second brother to Dr. Benjamin Borow. Louis was a radiologist. In the attic we had one room; it served as a bedroom, office, and sitting room. There was a small room with a sink and a Frigidaire, but no stove or oven. I prepared European-style gourmet meals on a hot plate and on a rotisserie. We shared a second-floor bathroom with Dr. and Mrs. Cutter and their young son. When one of us got up during the night, the other would ask, "Where are you going?" Considering the small quarters we had, it strikes us as funny today that we even thought there was any place to go besides our small room or the bathroom downstairs.

During the week Harvey worked at the hospital all day. I worked for Drs. Ben and Henry Borow, and I came home in the evenings and prepared our meals. On weekends we would go to Brooklyn to visit Harvey's parents unless he was on call. Our daughter, Tina, was conceived in that attic apartment in 1956 and was born on February 2, 1957, in Bound Brook Hospital. I worked through my whole pregnancy until the time of her birth. On the day of her birth there was a terrible snowstorm. I recall going to the hospital with labor pains on Thursday and having to wait until Saturday for Tina to be born. I was not dilating properly. One of Dr. Borow's associates, Dr. Albert Doswald, came in to examine me and decided to give me an injection to induce labor. This brought on excruciating pain. I could see Harvey turn snow white while he listened to my screams.

Dr. Ben Borow was finally summoned. He delivered Tina at 4 P.M. on Saturday afternoon. Harvey had wheeled me into the delivery room. I wondered how many husbands at that time had the chance to do that. Harvey was so shaken by the whole experience that he forgot to perform his chores as an X-ray technician. Before leaving work to be with me when the baby came, he literally forgot to put any film in the cassette in order to take the X-rays!

Once Tina was born, I was wheeled back into my room. Suddenly I felt the terrible void I had felt at my wedding, that of not having my father, but most especially my mother, with me. Not being able to partake of the happiness of having my newborn daughter "meet" her maternal grandparents, who I know would have loved and cherished her, was painful to me. Nevertheless, I found solace in the fact that my American family and the friends whom I considered my extended "family" responded so warmly.

Harvey's mother, father, sister, and brother-in-law, as well as my Aunt Minnie, came out to Bound Brook to help me. Beatrice Borow, who is sadly no longer alive, came to see me and brought baby clothes for a newborn child. Then there was Mary Rosenberg, an elderly member of the Bound Brook Temple, who came with a set of sterling silver cutlery. She said to me, "I hope this beautiful baby's life will be as beautiful as this shining sterling silver."

Ruth Kissel, who was the matriarch of the Jewish community in Bound Brook, came to see me. She embraced me as part of her own family. She was the best orator I knew. She never wrote her speeches or public presentations down, but spoke from her heart. She and her family were founders of the Bound

Brook Temple and oversaw the life of the Jewish community there. Another person who came to see me was Sylvia Adelberg. She was the president of the Bound Brook Temple Sisterhood, and she brought two gifts, one from the sisterhood and one from herself and her husband. The rabbi of the Bound Brook Temple was Hillel Horowitz. I remember that his wife, Faiga, baked cakes for the baby naming in temple on the first Sabbath that we could attend.

As much as I missed my parents and the other members of my family—aunts, uncles, and cousins—swallowed up in the Holocaust, I was comforted by the presence and participation in my life of those whom I am still proud to call my friends. They opened their arms and their hearts to me unconditionally.

Just before Tina was born, Harvey and I moved across the street to an apartment above Dr. Ben Borow's office. In that apartment I felt like royalty. I had a kitchen, a bathroom, and furniture of my own. We were able to furnish our dwelling to our taste. When I took Tina home, I took her to that apartment. My Aunt Minnie, Harvey's parents, and Harvey's sister and her family came out to help us and to be "introduced" to our new arrival. I also had a woman staying with me for a week who taught me the fundamentals of feeding, bathing, and caring for an infant. Yet I could not keep myself from thinking that had my mother been alive, I would have needed no one else. No one can take the place of a mother in a young woman's life, especially when she becomes a mother herself. Tina is named after my mother, Teresa Buchhalter.

# Family Present and Past

During the time following Tina's birth, I kept an immaculate house for my husband and did all I could to care for our baby. I did not return to work after she was born.

Throughout this pregnancy and my later one I took medications to maintain my resistance to tuberculosis and to avoid the possibility of a relapse. The medications made me lose my appetite, and I actually lost sixteen pounds during my first pregnancy. Whatever food I ate had to go toward nourishing the baby. Harvey was unable to take off from work, so I relied on the woman who was helping me. My weakened condition made it extremely difficult for me to take care of my child. My mother-in-law and my aunt came out to help care for us at that time.

Once I felt better, I would take Tina out in a carriage. We would go shopping, and on fair days would go for a stroll through the park. We had no car in those days. I remember vividly pushing the carriage up the hilly streets of Bound Brook on our return from the stores where we had shopped. The shopping area is in a valley, and there are hills on either side. Going up to the area around Church Street, where we lived, I found it extremely difficult to push the carriage, which contained not only Tina but also grocery parcels. But somehow I managed, occasionally with the help of others.

We became members of the Bound Brook Temple. I joined the Temple Sisterhood and made many friends. I was very fortunate that around this time Rosalee and Edward Borow (Dr. Ben's son) moved back to Bound Brook from Louisville, Kentucky, where they had been living. We immediately became very close friends. In fact, I thought of them as the brother and sister I had never had. At that time they had one child, Carol, about three or four years old. I watched Rosalee through her next four pregnancies, and the births of her sons, Mark, Philip, and Steven, and her daughter, Jill. We brought up our children together.

Eventually Maxwell Borow (Ben's other son) and his wife Eleanor also came back to Bound Brook. Maxwell, his brother, and some other doctors formed the Watchung Medical Group. Maxwell and Eleanor became another branch of my extended family. Their daughters Hilary and Leslie were also born when their parents returned to New Jersey. Maxwell and Eleanor had already had two children, Barbara and Elizabeth, and they also became good friends of my children. Through them we met another couple who became lifelong friends, Ann and Harold Yacowitz.

One day I was out walking with Tina in her carriage. A car pulled up with a young couple, Susan and Sheldon Guss. Sheldon was a pediatrician who was being interviewed for a place with the Watchung Medical Group. He was accepted. The Gusses and Harvey and I had a chemistry between us, and there arose the best friendship anyone could hope for. The care they extended to our family made a family of all of us. That care and friendship exists to this day. Susan and Sheldon had three sons, Bertram, Richard, and Howard. Sheldon was my children's pediatrician, and even my granddaughter's.

If I enumerate all these names, I have a reason, and for this reason it would be difficult to exclude any of them, as difficult as it would be to exclude any member of the American family I had discovered when I came here after the war. I had lost virtually every member of my immediate and extended European family in the fires of the Holocaust. I can only explain my finding all of these people as a mysterious but miraculous convergence of my need and their willingness to give me the help I needed. Through them I was able to recover from the horrors I had experienced, to rebuild my life, and to make whatever contribution I can make to the world's understanding of what happened to me and to so many others. I cherish them all.

In 1959 I became pregnant with my son, Joseph, and Harvey and I decided to go into business on our own. He left Bound Brook Hospital and opened his own laboratory, called Doctors' Medical Lab, at 567 Thompson Avenue in Bound Brook. We moved out of our apartment and into the Codrington Apartments, also in Bound Brook. Of course I became Harvey's helper. I did the books and the billing, and we built the business from the ground up. I typed reports and paid bills. He brought reports home at night, and I spent the evenings at the kitchen table typing them up. Joseph was born on January 29, 1960, at Somerset Hospital, now Somerset Medical Center. He was supposed to have been delivered by Dr. Albert Doswald, who had seen me through my nine months of pregnancy with my son. However, Dr. Doswald had to go home to Switzerland because of illness in his family, so Dr. John Wilson delivered Joseph. I admit that I had misgivings, but things worked out well anyway.

Joseph Samuel was named after my father, Joseph, and my father's younger brother, Samuel. When Joseph was born, Rosalee Borow couldn't be there with me, so she sent me a singing telegram that the delivery nurse sang to me during the hardest part of my labor.

On the day Joseph was born I'd gotten up early in the morning and cleaned our apartment thoroughly. I knew instinctively that this was the day on which I would give birth. Harvey didn't know that I was in labor, but at 10:30 I called him at work and asked him to take me to the hospital. They admitted me, took me upstairs, and examined me, and told him that there would be a long wait; they would call him at work to tell him I was about to deliver. No sooner did he get back to the laboratory than the phone rang, and he was informed that I had given birth to a baby boy. He went rushing back to the hospital.

After Joseph's birth, his coloring wasn't right, and he had to be put into an incubator. I wouldn't believe the doctors and nurses when they told me nothing was seriously wrong with him, and I thought something had happened to him. I carried on all night to such an extent that the next morning the nurse felt compelled to bring him to me as evidence that he was still alive and healthy.

As when Tina had been born, my relatives and Harvey's came to be with us after Joseph's birth. Since Tina was only three years old, Harvey took her to the hospital and held her literally under my window so that she could wave to me. I lifted up her baby brother to show him to her.

Once I was able to go home with Joseph, I returned to our little two-bedroom apartment on Union Avenue in Bound Brook. I hired a baby nurse for Joseph. The *bris*, the ceremony of circumcision, was held in the apartment. Before the *bris*, Eleanor Borow came to fix up the apartment. Joseph's godparents are Rosalee and Edward Borow.

The feeling I had with the birth of my second child was that my immediate family was complete again. My children were the link between the past and the future—the lost generation of the Holocaust and the new American family that Harvey and I had created. Joseph and Tina shared a room. Tina was a good sister. She sang songs to Joseph, and he never took his eyes off her.

In the Spring of 1962, when Joseph was two, our family moved into our very first house at 7 Woodlawn Road in Franklin Township. I fixed it up to look like a little doll's house. We did a good deal of entertaining. We remained close to our Bound Brook family, but we also joined the Jewish Community Center in Highland Park, where we enrolled our children in nursery school. While they were there, both of my children became very good swimmers and made many friends.

We stayed in Franklin Township until 1968 and then built our house at 121 Edgewood Drive in Bridgewater. Once we moved in there, I thought I was living in a mansion. Our children had many friends during their formative years, their adolescence, and their high school years. Tina and Joseph separated from their friends only after they had gone off to college.

Down the street from us lived Norbert and Gladys Schalet, who had two sons, Michael and Bennett. Joseph could not have been closer to these boys had they been his own brothers. Harvey's and my friendship with Norbert and Gladys was also close, particularly because Norbert was a Holocaust survivor. Gladys's immediate family had come from Hungary. They had arrived in America before World War II and settled in Philadelphia, but many of her extended family had perished in the Holocaust. With the Schalets I shared a special bond of memory.

Another person who played an important part in my family's life was the late Rabbi David Prince, who had officiated at my children's bar and bat Mitzvahs. I am still a very close friend of his wife, Lil, who calls me each Friday to wish me a joyous Shabbat. Those calls have always meant a great deal to me.

Both of my children were enrolled in the Bridgewater school system in 1968. I had not told them the terrible details of all my suffering during the Holocaust until they were teenagers, but they knew I had lost my entire family between 1944 and 1945. And they knew that all of this had happened because we were Jews. Tina and Joseph had each heard the stories at different times, and each had reacted differently.

Tina rarely spoke about it; she never asked direct questions or "acted out" her feelings about what she had heard. She rather tended to internalize the information until she went to college. She attended the University of Hartford. When she had to write essays, she always managed to insert stories about my experiences in the Holocaust. I learned of this only later and indirectly, because she never showed me her papers during that time. When Joseph was in college, he asked his sister if he could read her papers to get some ideas. She lent them to him, and he shared them with me. Although she could not speak to me directly about the things she had written, I believe she wanted me to be aware that she knew and understood.

Joseph was exactly opposite from his sister in the way he dealt with what I had told him. When he was about eight years old, he made a yellow Jewish star from paper and wrote *Jude* (Jew) on it. He wore it conspicuously on his outer clothing. He also engaged in several fistfights when other children made remarks about Jews. I was called to school on several occasions to discuss his behavior. At that time there was virtually no Holocaust education in the schools. But when I spoke to his teachers and explained my background to them and the reason for Joseph's emotional response, they understood and never punished him for fighting. He eventually matured emotionally and found other means through which to channel his feelings. Joseph graduated from Fairleigh Dickinson University at

Rutherford. He also graduated from the New York School for
Podiatry Medicine.

From my children I realized how difficult it must have been
for those of the Second Generation to deal with the experiences of their parents, particularly as they began to understand
the nature of what had happened. But I have never regretted
telling them what happened. I feel deeply that that knowledge
provided them with a coping strategy. They knew what happened rather than having to imagine the horror.

In 1972, shortly before Joseph's bar mitzvah, Harvey, our children, and I journeyed to Hungary, and from there to Israel.
Many of my fellow survivors from our land were making trips
back to where they were born at that time. I had seriously begun
thinking of doing likewise, but Harvey had opposed it at first.
He feared that the Communist government would keep us
there by force. The Cold War was, after all, still very much a
concern of the world. It might be easier for natives of a now-
Communist country to enter that country than to leave it. But
both Tina, fifteen, and Joseph, twelve, wished to know their
roots, and I wanted to see the only surviving relative from my
Hungarian family, my Uncle Henrik. I made arrangements, and
we left on June 23, 1972.

From the beginning our journey was fraught with anxiety.
We got to Kennedy Airport on a stormy day. The fields were so
wet that an incoming plane skidded off the tarmac, blocking all
incoming and outgoing flights. Our flight was delayed between
three and four hours. Harvey commented to me, "I told you we
shouldn't go."

We finally took off, flying on Swiss Air to Zurich. There
we were supposed to change to a smaller Swiss airplane that
would take us to Budapest. Prior to our take-off at Kennedy, I
had begun to fear that, because we had been delayed for over

four hours, we would miss our connecting flight. As soon as we boarded the plane, I asked for the head stewardess and expressed my nervousness to her. I requested that she suggest to the captain that he ask on the loudspeaker if anyone on the plane were possibly in the same predicament we were and feared missing the flight. He did so, and to my amazement, many others expressed the same concern. I then asked the stewardess to ask the captain to call ahead and request that our plane to Budapest be held until we got there. Since there were at least twenty other people on our flight in the same predicament, the captain complied, and the flight from Zurich to Budapest was held, pending our arrival. I am certain that the other passengers were probably wondering who the woman was who had opened her mouth on the flight out of Kennedy.

When we finally arrived in Zurich, I had but one mission. My Uncle Henrik had made me promise that I would buy a Swiss watch for him at the duty-free shop in the Zurich airport. Harvey and I had never purchased anything so fast, but we managed to accomplish our mission.

Once we boarded the plane for Hungary and our plane took off, I heard the Hungarian language being spoken by the stewardesses. My job of translating for Harvey and the children had immediately begun. I experienced an unnerving sense of déjà vu in the form of a migraine headache. I could feel myself being transported into a world I had all but forgotten and abandoned. I don't recall the length of the flight, but I remember our landing on the outskirts of the Firihegy Airport in Budapest and boarding a bus to take us to the terminal.

I was becoming an emotional basket case then and there. I got on the bus feeling apprehensive and physically upset. I went all the way to the last seats in the rear of the bus and crouched there, feeling that I wanted to hide from the world. As we approached the terminal, an aura of familiarity surrounded me.

Despite my nervousness on the bus, I wanted to prolong the bus ride to the terminal as long as possible. Harvey must have felt my sense of panic and dread. He said teasingly, "This was what you wanted, kiddo. It's time to face the music."

Suddenly I looked out at the place in the terminal where people were waiting for the passengers to debark from the bus, and at that moment I thought I saw my father's face! It was my Uncle Henrik, my father's brother, along with his wife, Bozske. I felt frozen in time. I remembered that I had had a similar feeling when I first saw my Aunt Minnie on the ship that had taken me to the United States. But eventually I had to get off the bus and "face the music." I waved to them.

Inside the customs area, agents were roughly but minutely going through everyone's luggage. I was anticipating that we might have difficulty going through the inspections. In contrast to most of our fellow passengers, who were dressed in drab and dark apparel, we wore clothing that was bright and of good quality and had clothes of the same type in our suitcases. When I spoke to the inspectors in Hungarian, they began to respond, bowing and speaking to us with almost excessive politeness, even kissing my hand. They must have thought we were royalty. I was both embarrassed and gratified. We went through inspection easily.

How does one prepare oneself for a family reunion that has taken twenty-eight years to become a reality? Old and new emotions welled up inside me in anticipation of being reunited with my uncle. I started to cry and tremble, and the migraine with which I had begun my journey increased in intensity. Yet I had to suppress my turbulent emotions for the sake of my husband and children. They looked at me with genuine anguish, as though they could read my feelings.

Finally I was reunited with my uncle. Falling into his arms and crying with him was an experience I cannot describe and will never forget. We had not seen each other in nearly thirty years. He had lost his wife and two little girls, and each of us had lost our entire family. We were the only survivors.

Harvey, Tina, and Joseph relied on my translation of my uncle's words, as neither he nor his wife spoke any English. After a while I became so ruffled at the task that I began speaking to my American family in Hungarian and to my uncle and his wife in English.

When we had gotten our luggage from the hand carriers, my uncle told me that I had overtipped them. We needed two cars for the six of us and all our luggage. Once our luggage was carried out, everyone appeared to be staring at it; probably no one was used to such bright reds amid the drab browns and blacks of Communist Hungary.

Our journey to the Hotel Intercontinental consisted largely of my Uncle Henrik's pointing out sights in Budapest with which, of course, I was not familiar. Once our hotel came into view, our children became excited, realizing that we were reaching our first destination. The hotel was in the heart of the city, on the Pest side near the Danube. It was luxuriously furnished and beautifully carpeted. But we could hardly wait to get upstairs, because we were physically exhausted and emotionally drained. I had reserved adjoining rooms for us and our children and for my uncle and his wife for our entire stay in Hungary. They had come up from Sarospatak to be with us during our sojourn.

We checked into the hotel, rested up, and went down to dinner. Everything was served family style. We had a delicious meal consisting of chicken broth with pieces of chicken and vegetables, followed by deep-fried chicken with *paprikash krumpli* (potatoes made with fried onions and paprika). There were also dumplings served with red *paprikash* sauce, a sweet salad made from Bibb lettuce, a cucumber salad, and mixed vegetables. All of this glorious food was served on Herend china (Hungary is famous for its fine china). We ended our meal with a dessert of Hungarian pastries, then washed the meal down with Hungarian wine. Our meal was accompanied by delightful gypsy music vocalized by a beautiful Hungarian girl. Meanwhile, my translation was going back and forth

After dinner we went into the lobby to talk, as the hotel rooms seemed too small. My uncle wanted to know everything about our Hungarian family, particularly about the deportation, all the camps I had been in, and with whom. After a while, we felt we had to go upstairs. Our emotions were far too powerful for a public place. In our room I tried to explain to Henrik everything that had happened to me during the last twenty-eight years. Even in the privacy of our room, with Harvey, the children, and Henrik's wife there, our emotions were too extreme for us to deal with calmly. We started to cry and held onto one another.

Henrik kept stroking and caressing my children and repeating my father's name over and over again. He "spoke" to my father and to the rest of the family, tearfully telling my father that he was with his daughter and grandchildren. Harvey wanted me to translate what Henrik was saying, but in a way I was actually glad that he was speaking Hungarian; it was too much for me emotionally to attempt an English translation of what Henrik was trying to express, and at the moment it seemed most bearable to keep what he and I were saying to one another to ourselves.

Finally, Henrik and his wife went to their room. My original plan had been to have Tina stay with Harvey and me and Joseph to stay with my uncle and his wife. But I now insisted on keeping both children in the same room with Harvey and me. I had an irrational fear of letting go of them. My fear had nothing to do with Henrik, as I tried to explain to him. I simply could not let my children go.

The next morning, while we were still asleep, a strange thing happened. My uncle had apparently bribed a chambermaid to let him into our room. When we awoke, we found him at the foot of our bed, kissing our children's feet. As odd as this behavior might seem, even in retrospect, I am certain of the meaning of what was happening. He was both reliving his experience of loss and clinging to our children as a connection to the future, the future from which he had been cut off by the murder of his own little girls. The children were puzzled, but all I could do was tell them of what he had lost and what our presence in Hungary meant to him.

During the second day of our stay in Budapest, we walked together through the streets of the city. Henrik, Bozske, and I went side by side, while Harvey walked ahead with the children. It seemed eerie, this feeling of ordinary everyday life that we experienced in walking through a place where, less than three decades earlier, Jews had been rounded up for deportation.

On the third day, we left Budapest. We hired a van and a driver to take us to the area where I had lived. Before beginning the trip, and with no knowledge of our driver's political views and affiliations or his ability to understand English, we instructed the children and each other not to say anything derogatory about Hungary or about the Soviet occupation.

The first major stop we made en route was in Miskolc. My father used to purchase supplies there for his general store and prayed in the synagogue. I had spent wonderful vacation times there with my cousins. When the van stopped, Joseph stayed with my aunt and the rest of us went into the store, the inventory of which was very sparse, although we found beautiful tablecloths. There was a scarcity of merchandise in virtually every store we entered, and the explanation we were given everywhere was that "inventory" was being taken.

Meanwhile, Joseph and my aunt found the synagogue where my father had prayed. When we rejoined them we entered the synagogue. The shammes (sexton) came over to us to greet us. At one point Joseph ran over to the *bimah* (the raised platform in the middle of the synagogue) and began praying. At this time he was in the process of preparing for his bar mitzvah, but it almost seemed to us that some force had impelled him to run over to the platform and begin praying at the top of his lungs. The shammes was gratified to see a young Jew practicing his faith. This probably seemed for the older man a sign that Judaism was being reborn. Before leaving, we gave him some money for the upkeep of the synagogue.

From Miskolc we proceeded through Tolcsva to Horvati, my father's hometown. We passed through the vineyards that my family had owned. The rush of familiarity I suddenly experienced was not easy on my nerves. We went through town to the grave of my paternal grandfather. Everything was muddy—it had rained the day before. We could not find a tombstone. My uncle took us to a spot that he said was the gravesite. He explained that during the war the Jewish cemetery had been leveled. There we recited the Kaddish, the prayer of sanctification that is said for the dead, and we cried.

When the people of the area saw us, they came out with flowers and talked with me. Even the geese were following me. The older people mistook me for my father's sister, my Aunt Elizabeth, with whom I had gone through the horrors of the camps. They knew my uncle, who had been through the town many times since the war. Those who had been my father's contemporaries even remembered him, but I wanted only to get out as quickly as I could. When my uncle told them who I was, shock came over their faces. Were they possibly wondering how I survived? My emotions were probably extreme, but I truly wanted to get away from there. I didn't want to hear their voices! Where had they been when my family had been taken away? Their "geniality" and "friendliness" now upset me; I saw it as hypocrisy.

We got back into the van and proceeded to Tolcsva. We passed the school I had attended, and I stopped momentarily in the schoolyard, where Harvey took photographs. We then got back into the van and drove into the heart of Tolcsva. I could not recognize anything; there was no synagogue and no Jewish stores.

We made a left turn into the street where my family's house still stood. We looked around; I noticed a familiar brook, but nothing else was recognizable to me. I looked at the house in which we had lived. I saw pigs, goats, and chickens running around. The yard was completely different from what it had once been. Our feet were covered with mud. I took off the children's shoes and my shoes, and we washed the shoes in the basin of water underneath the water pump.

The people who lived there came out and peered at us curiously. My uncle explained to them why I was there. The people were polite. I asked myself, "Why am I torturing myself in coming here? Of what benefit to me is it to return, if nothing is as I remember it?"

Tina wanted to go inside to see the rooms, but I wouldn't. I couldn't cross the threshold. Nothing looked or smelled as it once had. I walked around the outside. I saw peach trees, I saw barns. Did I want to see neighbors? my uncle asked. Definitely not, I replied emphatically.

I wanted only to go to the cemetery to visit the grave of my other grandfather. The cemetery was virtually in ruins, but my grandfather's headstone was still sufficiently intact for me to recognize it. I went up to the stone and embraced it. Suddenly

I was seized with the realization that there were no other graves belonging to any of my relatives. At that moment I felt faint and virtually passed out. Joseph and Tina came running over to me, crying "Mommy, Mommy, please stop this!" Harvey also reacted protectively and held me. I tried to compose myself. I spoke to my grandfather across the boundaries of time, of life and death. I said to him, "At least you have a resting place, and a marker for your gravesite, unlike the rest of your family, who perished in the flames of Auschwitz!"

Then I calmed down. My uncle, my immediate family, and I said the Kaddish, and then we left.

We went on to Sarospatak, to the apartment of my uncle and my aunt. A shock of remembrance hit me again when we got there. We saw furniture belonging to my father's brother; we saw rugs that I suddenly recalled from my childhood. There were other mementos, some of which my uncle offered to me. But I didn't want to take anything. I hadn't the heart for it.

We had tea, and then we went down into the wine cellar, where we tasted some of the delicious Hungarian wine that I also recalled from earlier days. At my uncle's insistence I finally took six cups and saucers of Hungarian china. Those had been wedding presents given at his first marriage. At the end of the war, Henrik had been in Dachau. When he returned to Hungary, he took whatever he found of family possessions and heirlooms. Most of these were very old. We realized how old they were when at one point Harvey sat down in a chair that literally collapsed under his weight. Henrik and Bozske had lived for many years with these mementos of our departed family.

We could not stay with my uncle and aunt, as they had only a small one-bedroom apartment. That night we stayed in a hotel in Sarospatak that used to be a monastery. We had to leave our passports with the hotel management overnight. Harvey was fearful that our passports would not be returned to us or that some calamity would befall us, given the fact that I was originally of Hungarian nationality. All four of us stayed in one room. I would not let my children out of my sight.

The rooms were small, with little bunk beds. I also remember a sink. The children slept in their own bunk beds. I slept in the same bunk bed with Harvey, holding onto him the entire night. It was probably the worst night of the trip, and I was very anxious to leave that region of Hungary.

The next day, to our relief, we got our passports back. On the road back to Budapest I sat in my usual front seat of the car, next to the driver, since I was the one translating for everyone. Suddenly I realized that an official car was following us, with its lights flashing. Our van was pulled over by gendarmes. Harvey immediately became apprehensive. "They had your passport. They know who you are. They are probably coming for you!" In the confusion, my uncle took over, and explained to me what was going on. In the car were a high official and his wife who were on their way to the airport and in a hurry. Our driver had not extended the requisite courtesy to an officer's car by allowing it to pass. Furthermore, the driver didn't want to apologize. Finally I apologized for him, and we were permitted to drive on. We drove through the Black Mountains and stopped at a restaurant for a meal. For a little while, I could recover from the anguish of the preceding day. Having our meal together amid the beautiful mountain scenery and being able to distance myself from my town and the experience of the day before did much to soothe me. We then continued our journey to Budapest.

I wanted to spend the upcoming Sabbath in Budapest. I wanted to attend the magnificent Dohany Street Synagogue for Sabbath services. I informed my uncle of that fact and invited him to join us, which he consented to do. I also wanted to make arrangements for us to have a traditional Sabbath meal together on Friday night. However, I was unable to arrange this because arrangements with and payments to the kosher restaurant in Budapest would have had to be made in advance of our ability to do so. So we had to content ourselves with an ordinary meal in the hotel restaurant.

The next morning we attended services. The liturgical part of the service was conducted, of course, in traditional Hebrew, but the spoken part was in Hungarian. I was glued to my seat and virtually hypnotized by both parts of the service because of what it meant to me to realize that Hitler's ambitions of obliterating Hungarian Jewry had not been realized. That remnant of Jewry who had survived and returned to reclaim their homes and lives on their native soil was thriving! For me it was thrilling to hear the Jewish faith expressed through my mother tongue and rejuvenating to know that *Yiddishkeit* (Jewish life and customs) was alive in Hungary again.

Afterward we toured the synagogue grounds, especially the Jewish cemetery. The cemetery was on the spot where in 1944 Budapest Jews had been shot and killed by the Nazis, and their names were visible on plaques. In the back of the synagogue we saw *Yahrzeit* (memorial) candles that had been lit for the dead and food that was being prepared to feed the homeless and the needy. Mindful of the deaths that had taken place on these grounds, the saving Jewish remnant of Budapest showed its concern for the living in need. What greater lesson of our enduring faith could I teach my children?

When the ten days of our tour were over, my aunt and uncle went with us to the airport, and there we said our goodbyes. Saying goodbye was not easy. We all cried and embraced and held onto each other. It was hard for me to leave my uncle and aunt there. My Aunt Minnie and I had always hoped to persuade Henrik and his wife to come to the United States, but he had always refused. How different their lives might have been if they had accepted our plea!

My Uncle Henrik died on May 30, 1973, less than a year after our reunion. I feel now that it was intended for me to make that trip so that I could see him one last time. My Aunt Bozske died in July of 1995.

# 10

# *Israel*

---

The airplane took us back to Zurich. We stayed in a hotel at the airport. While there we contacted Dr. Harvey Sudson, the son of Goldie and Lou Sudson, friends who lived in Piscataway, New Jersey. He was studying medicine in Zurich. We visited with him, and he kindly took us around the city.

The next morning we left for Israel, and many hours later we landed in Tel Aviv. I remember feeling truly at home aboard the plane. I was among my own people, and I no longer felt helpless and homeless. We went through customs, and then took a taxi through Tel Aviv to our hotel. Our tour had been arranged through the Israel Bonds organization, for which I work as a volunteer. They took care of the sightseeing on our trip.

After a day or two in beautiful, modern Tel Aviv visiting the Museum of the Diaspora and Tel Aviv University, as well as the city's lovely hotels and beach areas, we traveled to Netanya, where we met with some local friends whom we knew from Bound Brook, the late Hyman and Helen Stallman. Hyman had been active in soliciting money for United Jewish Appeal in New Jersey, and they had made *aliyah*, that is, settled in Israel. The food in Israel was very poor at that time, and we had our first decent meal at the Stallman home.

While in Netanya, a seashore resort that goes back to Roman times, we tried to go swimming, but as we walked on the sand our feet got covered with black tar, probably from oil deposits. The natives must have been used to this, because as we left the beach we found a scrub brush and some liquid to remove the tar.

In Jerusalem, as part of the Israel Bond tour we went everywhere. In contrast to my early experience as a Jew, which had been marked by restriction, oppression, cruelty, and being made to feel an outsider, in this city I felt completely free and at home. Harvey and Joseph went to visit the caves. Tina and I went to visit orphanages and homes for the elderly, both of which interested me. These are types of institutions with which I am still involved today at home. I had realized long before how vulnerable and helpless the very young and the elderly had been in the Holocaust, and my dream was to increase the well-being of both segments of the population. I was particularly impressed with the way in which the Israelis treated the elderly. These people were engaged in activities and in fulfilling their interests. They were not allowed to vegetate or stagnate.

We also went to Masada and the Dead Sea. Masada is a mountaintop fortress where the Jews resisted captivity by the Romans and committed mass suicide rather than submitting to Roman rule and the betrayal of their faith. Harvey imagined that we were "walking through the Bible."

The week that we spent in Israel in the summer of 1972 provided a kind of medicine for me. It was a year before the Yom Kippur War, and the euphoria of the 1967 War could still be felt throughout the nation. The trauma of anticipating and experiencing my return to Hungary gradually dissolved in Eretz Yisroel (the Land of Israel) amid the vibrancy and hopefulness Harvey and I both felt both because we were in the land of our people and because of my own sense of belonging somewhere.

I went back to Israel in 1981 for the first World Gathering of
the Jewish Holocaust Survivors. Harvey was supposed to accompany me on this trip, but to my disappointment he could not
because of business complications. I took Joseph with me
instead; he was then twenty-one.

Susan Guss and her son, Howard, took us to Kennedy Airport. We arrived only to be told that we were not listed as being
on the El Al flight. After the airline had taken Harvey's name
off the list, they had assigned his seat to someone else, and they
refused to substitute Joseph's name for his. I did not want to
travel alone. An hour later our travel agent arrived, and she took
us over to Alitalia. With the help of the travel agent we were
both booked on Flight 1601, which left at 7:30 P.M. for Milan.

Flying from Kennedy to Milan, we saw the French Alps
with their snow-capped tips. It was a magnificent sight to
behold! We had an hour's layover in Milan, and then a forty-
minute flight to Rome. In Rome we stayed two hours, and then
boarded another Alitalia flight to Tel Aviv. As we were taxi-
ing out to the runway, we had a power failure and had to taxi
back to the terminal, where we waited for the crew aboard the
plane to correct the situation. By now all seventy-two of us
bound for Israel were thoroughly exhausted, and we were still
facing a three-hour flight to our destination.

On June 12 (my fifty-second birthday) at 9 P.M. we finally
arrived at Ben Gurion Airport. We were greeted there with
bouquets of flowers and TV cameras. Then we were bussed to
our hotel, the Diplomat. Once Joseph and I checked into the
hotel and were greeted by survivor friends, the Frisches, from
my community, we put our luggage in our hotel room and we
went down to find some food.

The change in atmosphere in Israel between 1972 and 1981
was indeed dramatic. Joseph and I found a bazaarlike area filled
with shops and food courts emitting a delicious aroma. I can

still taste the St. Peter's fish, which tastes nowhere as delicious as in Israel (Joseph, true to his American heritage, was content to have his hamburger and french fries). As we were eating our food we could only contrast it with the awful food we had to put up with in 1972. Things had changed for the better!

The next day, Saturday, was a day of rest, and we spent much of it at the hotel pool with the Frisches. In the evening we went to a restaurant called Ketan in Dizengoff Street. There I had the most delicious Sabbath meal of *cholent* with roast goose, which took me back to my childhood in Hungary.

On Sunday morning, June 14, buses arrived at the hotel decorated with banners welcoming Holocaust survivors for the world gathering in Jerusalem. Our tour guide was Haim Beth Ativa, and our bus driver's name was Mordecai Motka. We left Tel Aviv for Ashdod and the ancient city of Jaffa, which is now known for its great outdoor markets, which we went through. Haim was an excellent guide. He took us on new highways in a southerly direction. We saw beautiful new buildings, power plants, and the new port of Ashdod. Haim told us that the port had been built in nine years.

We then visited Esqulen and Yad Mordecai. We stopped at a rest place called Heide Rana, where we saw young soldiers, both boys and girls, who were smiling and friendly and posed willingly with us for pictures. One was holding a white rabbit and playing with it. Seeing the young soldiers, male and female, riding the buses from one place to another and dependent on this mode of transportation, I made up my mind that I would one day return to Israel, buy a bus, and spend my time doing nothing but chauffeuring them around wherever they had to go.

We went to a kibbutz called El Mordecai. There we saw a model battlefield from the Yom Kippur War of 1973, still set up with wooden soldiers representing the Egyptian army, their rifles in hand, and with model trucks, airplanes, tanks, and trenches.

We saw also the underground shelter. There is a plaque there bearing an inscription that included the words of Mordecai Anielewicz, the heroic leader of the Warsaw Ghetto Uprising: "My life's last wish is fulfilled. The Independent Jewish Resistance has come through. I am happy to be amongst the first Jewish fighters in the Ghetto." This statement is dated April 23, 1943.

Late in the afternoon we returned to our hotel. My most urgent mission at the time was to arrange our return flight on El Al, making certain that Joseph and I were both booked on the same plane. Later we went to a Hungarian restaurant called Nes Ziona, where we had a delicious Hungarian meal.

After dinner we went to a reception hosted by the city of Tel Aviv and held at its Yad Eliahu Sports Stadium. It was sponsored by the World Federation of Jewish Fighters, Partisans, and Camp Inmates. Being under the same roof with so many of our fellow survivors produced a sense of euphoria. We felt like members of a gigantic family, sharing stories, embracing, and kissing one another though we didn't know one another.

On June 15 we left for Jerusalem. Joseph and the Frisches and I went in a private car, because there was not enough room for all of us on the bus. One thing disturbed me deeply. As we were waiting (in vain) to board the bus, people were pushing and shoving and jostling one another, and one could not help but be reminded of the hoards of people pushing and jostling in the camps in order to be first for food. It may not be rational, but to many survivors even the most innocuous situations trigger memories of the camps.

Our first stop on the way to Jerusalem was at the Museum of the Diaspora. We could have spent hour upon hour there, but my first mission was to go to go to the computer and see if I could obtain any news of my Hungarian town or community. The only name that came up was Satoraljaujhely. I learned that about 4,000 Jews had been deported from Satoraljaujhely in the spring of 1944. Of these, only 555 survived. There were 204 Jews living there in 1953.

After we left the museum we proceeded to Jerusalem, and I could not help marveling at the changes that had taken place in the roads, buildings, and general landscape since my last visit in 1972. The roads were wider and more congested, and there were more buildings and settlements dotting the landscape.

At 6 p.m. we went to the opening ceremony of the World Gathering of Holocaust Survivors, which was held at Yad Vashem. We heard from Israeli President Yitzhak Navon. Before departing from our homelands each of us had been asked to bring with us a stone with the name of a lost loved one inscribed on it. Harvey and I had had a discussion about this, and we had decided to buy a piece of marble such as one uses for tombstones. I had my parents' names inscribed on it, and during the opening ceremony I handed it in at the time when each of us was asked to hand in our stone to Yad Vashem to be placed in a Wall of Remembrance. I must say that this ceremony gave me a sense of closure and inner peace; I knew that, although my parents lacked a gravesite, there was finally a place we could come to "be with" our loved ones, at least in spirit, and to say the Kaddish.

Although the speakers spoke movingly and the ceremony was very powerful, there were no seats, the air was quite chilly, and my emotions were so worked up that Joseph insisted on taking me back to my hotel. There I had to call my husband, whom I missed very much at that moment, to speak with him and have a good cry.

On Tuesday, June 16, we visited the Old City and the Arab marketplaces, where merchants plied their wares in individual stalls that lined the long, narrow corridors of stone between buildings. In the late afternoon we visited the survivors' kibbutz,

Netzer Sereni, one hour away from Jerusalem. We had our first kibbutz meal, and then we toured the kibbutz. We observed their furniture manufacturing and saw examples of their farming, which took me back to my childhood. We also examined their bomb shelters. In short, we saw briefly the daily life of the very brave and resourceful people who had chosen this way of life.

The Netzer Sereni kibbutz had an interesting history. It was located near the towns of Ramlat and Rehovot, and its members had come from many parts of Europe (Eastern and Western) as well as Morocco, Syria, India, Egypt, Yemen, and Iraq. The kibbutz had been conceived right after the liberation of Buchenwald and Bergen-Belsen (at first it was even called Kibbutz Buchenwald). The survivors had settled on the site in June 1948. It had once been the site of a German school for Arab orphans, and later of the headquarters for the British Army in the First World War. The word *Netzer* refers to a branch sprouting from a tree trunk, and Sereni is for Enzo Sereni, an Italian-Jewish pioneer who, like the better-known Hannah Senesh, parachuted behind German lines to rescue Jews and was captured and murdered in Dachau.

The next day we traveled to a Second Generation meeting at Binyanei HaOoma in Jerusalem. I wanted Joseph to meet some other members of the Second Generation, children of Holocaust survivors. He sat and listened attentively, but said little. From there we went to the computer area to look for information about our families' fates. Everywhere we went we met people holding up pieces of cardboard with names written on them on. Following each name was a question mark. These people still did not know what had happened to their relatives. They seemed to be appealing to us with their eyes to give them information that we did not have.

In the evening, thanks to our friends the Roswells, we attended a concert by the American composer Marvin Hamlisch, who at the time was touring Israel. After the concert he gave a private reception at the Hotel King David, which we attended as well, and we chatted briefly with him. This provided us with a respite from all the stressful and emotional events we had experienced during our three days at the gathering.

The next day we attended a dedication of the Jerusalem Great Synagogue at Heichal Shlomo in memory of the six million people who had perished in the Holocaust. At 4 P.M. we assembled at the Zion Gate for a procession to the Western Wall. This wall, the only part of the ancient Jewish Temple to survive destruction in 70 C.E. by the Romans, is a sacred site for Jews, where they pray and leave petitions on tiny pieces of paper that they wedge into crevices between its ancient stones. At the wall at least five thousand people were assembled. The Frisches and we sat on the hill to the right of the wall so that we could have a good view of the proceedings. It was an impressive sight to behold. I was gratified both to be there with my son and to be part of this event with my fellow survivors. I wished desperately that my husband and daughter could have been there with us, because only that way could one fully appreciate it.

At the entrance to the *kotel* (the area surrounding the Western Wall) each of us was given a *Yahrzeit* candle to light in memory of our loved ones. Suddenly something extraordinary happened that could only have happened in Israel: a bridal party, with the bride still in her gown, came marching down to the wall. Probably they were coming for a blessing. In the midst of this solemn ceremony, a place was made to acknowledge the cycle of life and to remind us of life's joys even as we remembered the sorrow and pain of death.

The organizer of the World Gathering, Ernst Michel, spoke. Then the rabbi of the *kotel* said some prayers. Benjamin Mead, chairman of the evening program, also offered some words. Menachem Begin gave a gut-wrenching speech that made the rafters shake with applause. He talked of his camp experiences, the shedding of Jewish blood. He promised us that it would never happen again, and he spoke of Israel as the only buffer against another Holocaust.

Then there was a prayer for the dead. The closing portion consisted of a recitation of the "Pledge of Acceptance by the Second Generation of the Legacy of the Holocaust Survivors." It was read in six languages: Hebrew, English, Yiddish, French, Russian, and Ladino. As darkness set in, six candles, one for each million of the six million, were lit. The ceremony ended with the singing of "Jerusalem, City of Gold," which was written after Israel regained in Jerusalem in the 1967 War.

The next day Joseph and I left the hotel for our flight home. On our way to the airport I wrote down my thoughts in the hope that I would someday put them in a more finished form.

The flight home was long and uneventful, but I had an extraordinary experience when we arrived at Kennedy Airport. Harvey had been attending the wedding of the Gusses oldest son, Bertram. He had left right after the ceremony, and although he never drives anywhere by himself, he headed out to Kennedy to meet us at the plane. I was shocked, entering the reception area, to see him standing there. He shouted out to me in front of everyone, "I'm here to pick up my bride!" I was never so happy to see anyone in my life. We made a pledge to each other never to travel again without one another.

The World Gathering was not a happy occasion for me, but it was an exalting one. It made me aware of the necessity of bringing Holocaust survivors together so that we might not only find support for ourselves within our own group, but also empower ourselves to pass the legacy of the Holocaust down to future generations by educating each generation about its horrors and about the positive lessons that can be learned from it: lessons of decency, tolerance, moral responsibility, and social justice.

In subsequent years I attended other survivor gatherings in Washington, 1983; Philadelphia, 1985; New York, 1991; and Miami Beach, 1995. All were powerful, combining painful memories with catharsis, but none affected me as deeply as the one in Israel in 1981.

# 11

# *A Mission*

---

$\mathbf{T}$ina graduated from the University of Hartford in 1979 with a bachelor's degree in communication arts. After Joseph graduated from high school, he attended the University of Miami and then Fairleigh Dickinson University in Rutherford, New Jersey, from which he graduated in 1982, and the New York College of Podiatric Medicine, from which he received a D.P.M. in 1986.

Watching my children achieve what I could not achieve in my youth allowed me to reflect on my own youth through them. I could experience vicariously what I had not, because of the Holocaust, been able to experience in fact. While they were in college my thirst for knowledge was so profound that I felt compelled to enroll in the Bound Brook High School adult program, where I took classes and got my high school diploma in October 1979. At the commencement exercises I was given the honor of welcoming the guests.

Once I was graduated I felt I had acquired a better grasp of the English language. This gave me the incentive to become more involved in my community. I became the president of my temple sisterhood, and after that I became one of the vice presidents of Temple Knesset Israel's board of trustees. Then I became involved in the Jewish Federation of Somerset, Warren, and Hunterdon Counties. I was first a federation board member and then president. I am also a life member of the local Council of Jewish Women and of the Somerset chapter of Hadassah. I chaired both the Israel Bonds campaign and the United Jewish Appeal in Somerset County.

While I was involved in the federation I served as vice president of the board of the Somerset County Jewish Family Service, which I was instrumental in helping to establish. I also served on the board of directors of Somerset County Family Services. I am still a vice president of the Central New Jersey Jewish Home for the Aged. My goals in doing community work have had little to do with self-aggrandizement or recognition. I have had three other reasons for serving: to give something back to my community for the love and respect they had shown to me from the time I had settled in the area, to help better the lives of my Jewish brothers and sisters, and finally to challenge myself to show the world that I, a person who had been robbed by murderous genocide of virtually every personal possession and relationship, could rebuild my life and help to lead a community of my fellow Jews.

One area that has deeply concerned me in recent years, even more than most others, has been the absence of awareness of the situations of aging Holocaust survivors. I had been pushing very hard to create a program that might meet their particular needs. These people were dealing with the dual problems of aging and of the trauma with which they were still forced to cope. I was aware that as survivors age and become more dependent on others, there are numerous triggers in their environment that can cause them to recall frightening and painful memories. Yet there had been little, if any, movement to heighten the sensitivities of caregivers to the particular problems of the survivors themselves, many of whom had lost entire families and were still wounded both psychologically and physically.

On May 4, 1995, the Central New Jersey Jewish Home for the Aged, with which I am affiliated, offered a workshop for nurses, nurse's aides, and other caregivers of geriatric Holocaust survivors. Prior to the workshop we took several busloads of these caregivers to the Holocaust Museum in Washington, D.C., in order to acquaint them with the history of the Holocaust and with the suffering endured by the people for whom they were caring.

The workshop itself featured Dr. Yehuda Nir, an associate professor of psychiatry at Cornell University and a psychiatrist at New York Hospital. Dr. Nir was also the author of a memoir, *The Lost Childhood,* in which he had recounted his experience as a nine-year-old in Poland during the war years. He was also a psychiatrist for the Hassidic Satmar communities in Williamsburg, Brooklyn, and Monroe, New York. Both Williamsburg and Monroe have large numbers of Holocaust survivors and Second Generation members. Other speakers at this workshop included representatives from the U.S. Holocaust Museum and Toby Kansagor, an educator who is also part of the Second Generation.

I met and worked with many outstanding people during my years of community service, but I must single out two very dear friends of mine: Betty and Arthur Roswell. Betty's family was from Baltimore, and her father's name was Jacob Blaustein. He was instrumental in helping to establish vehicles for making restitution to the Holocaust survivors from Germany. By way of thanks, the Holocaust survivors of Bergen-Belsen presented him with a gold-leaf book, *Holocaust and Rebirth.* In 1992, when Betty and Art were closing down her late father's library, she came across the book. She and Art decided then and there to present the book to me with these words:

To Our Dear Friend Margit:

It's our privilege to give you this book from Dad's library, knowing that you will carry on the work to make certain that the world will always remember.

Betty and Art

When I received this book, for several hours daily I locked myself into my home office and, for a period of two weeks, read the text, looked at the pictures, cried, and remembered my life in Bergen-Belsen. I found in the book a picture of myself taken at the time of our liberation by the British. How much this book has meant to me Betty and Art can never know. My subconscious mind had locked away large portions of my experience in Bergen-Belsen. Reading this book helped to jog my memory and to recall our life-in-death existence. It also made me remember the liberation more clearly. Through this book my fellow inmates who perished in Bergen-Belsen live in me as I speak of them in my lectures and remember them in my thoughts.

My involvement with Holocaust lecturing goes back to a much earlier time, the mid-1970s. Rosalie and Edward Borow's son Philip was attending Bound Brook High School. I was a constant visitor at the Borow house. In fact, I regarded it as my second home. I always engaged in conversation with Philip. He was a very mature young man who wanted to be a lawyer. He was the most inquisitive of their children, and one of the subjects he prodded me to talk about most was my Holocaust experience.

On the other hand, he would consistently ask me, "Am I upsetting you? Please let me know." Often I began to cry, and Rosalie would scold him, "Please, Philip, leave Margit alone! Don't you see what this is doing to her?" My own response was. "It's all right. Let him ask." As painful as it was for me, the telling of what had happened produced a release of emotion that I had until then repressed.

After discussing things with his family, one day Philip brought this release to the next level. He called me and said, "Aunt Margit, please come to my school and talk to the students about the Holocaust. They need to know."

I was certain I could not face the experience of telling my story in public, and I said no. I became emotionally paralyzed, not only at the thought of having to reveal my emotional stress in recounting my experiences, but also at my self-consciousness in facing a class of American adolescents. My English was foreign sounding; my pronunciation was shaky. I still found it difficult to articulate certain thoughts. But Philip didn't give up. One day he came over with a tape recorder and made me tell my story into it. Then he took it in to school, and the students, he told me, listened intently to the narrative and were greatly affected by it. In a letter he wrote to the coauthor of this book on October 16, 1998, Philip, now an attorney, described the context and effect on the class of hearing my tape:

> Entering Junior High School is a period of changing self-consciousness and awareness. I was preparing for my Bar Mitzvah and I was experiencing my first incidents of anti-Semitism. It was during that time that I took an English course with a teacher by the name of Mrs. Roth. She was a tough talking young Jewish woman from Brooklyn. I was one of two Jewish students in the class, and one of a handful in the entire school. Mrs. Roth assigned the class the task of reading *The Diary of Anne Frank*. Each day, Mrs. Roth would assign the class a new selection to read. The following day, she would have the students take on roles and read aloud the assigned selection. Although I was a quiet student, I was a very active participant in this particular exercise.

One day I asked my Aunt Margit if she would be willing to recount her experiences into a tape recorder to be played to my class. I sat down with her while she spoke, listening to stories I had never heard before. By some odd quirk the original tape broke, and I had to ask Aunt Margit to do it a second time, for which I remain filled with embarrassment to this day.

I brought the tape into school and played it to our class. After the class there was simple silence. I think many of the students were struck by hearing from someone about what probably happened to Anne Frank after she was caught, someone who had been about the same age as we were when she experienced these things. I remember Aunt Margit telling how she never saw her parents again, how people were randomly killed just because they were there, how they were horribly treated. I remember thinking about the parallels between my Aunt Margit and Anne Frank, and that this woman in front of me had been a young girl and experienced all of this at my age. Not many students ever said much about the tape to me, and many seemed almost to feel embarrassed about it, but I know that not many will ever forget what they heard.

As time went on, however, I began thinking about speaking to a group. I like to believe that I am my own best "psychiatrist." I reason things out with myself and come, hopefully, to the right conclusion. My fellow survivor Gerda Klein often mentions in her lectures that today's parents, whenever their children are disturbed by anything, take them to psychiatrists or psychotherapists. "But where were our therapists when we were liberated?" she asks. The fact is that many of us were forced to survive on our own—and did manage to do so. Despite the fragmentation of our lives and the wounds that will never heal, we managed to reestablish ourselves in the world of the living, and we did so largely alone. So I always tend to weigh the pros and cons of everything myself and do what I think is ultimately right.

From the day Philip told me of the students' reaction to the tape of my story, I was determined that I would go in person to lecture to schools, colleges, and adult groups about the Holocaust, based upon my own experience of it. I realized that others, particularly young people, needed to know what we survivors had endured and what we had lost. I began a process that I continue to this day.

In the beginning, I found the experience horrendous. My English was poor. I felt self-conscious and nervous about either not finding or mispronouncing the appropriate words. I also feared also that in recalling the torture and humiliation of those days, I would relive it all mentally. However, I learned early to deal with these feelings. I had to discipline myself not to break down or to falter, particularly when telling of the loss of my family. However hard it was in those early days, I persevered.

As time went on, I developed a shield that I use today to separate my emotional self from the presentation. I block out from my mind certain events too painful to remember. I simply close my eyes frequently during my presentation and visualize what I want to say. I have no "technique." I'm open, loving, caring. I speak from the heart. I try to maintain a soft voice throughout. When I speak about the silence of the world, which is my major theme, I speak from pain, not anger. I feel hurt. Hurt is not hate.

With children in particular I say, "You are your brothers' keepers; every one of you is God's child." I ask young people, particularly those from fourteen to sixteen, to visualize themselves as me at that age and to imagine going through what I went through. I also use the fact that Anne Frank and I were born on the same day in the same year and were both in Bergen-

Belsen at about the same time. Thus I could be speaking for her and for all the other people of that age who perished.

I travel extensively in and around the state of New Jersey. I lecture to somewhere between forty and forty-five schools per academic year and have received thousands of letters from students. I have also done videotapes for collections at Yale University, Kean College, Yad Vashem, and the Spielberg Foundation.

In 1980 President Jimmy Carter appointed the first Holocaust Memorial Council, which was approved unanimously by Congress. In 1981 a telephone call came from Eileen McCoy, dean of community education and services at Raritan Valley Community College, to the Jewish Federation of Somerset County. She had received a letter from President Ronald Reagan, as had thousands of other college administrators around the United States, requesting that colleges across the country hold a "day of remembrance" of the Holocaust. She had immediately begun looking for a speaker to help organize a program for a Yom Ha'Shoah (Holocaust Remembrance Day). In turn, the federation office called me, and I was invited to meet with Eileen McCoy. At that meeting was a professor of anthropology, Dr. Steven Kaufman, who was active at the college in seeing that religious diversity was observed and had personally lost members of his extended family in the Holocaust. I was asked, as a survivor, to be the Holocaust spokesperson.

The speech I gave at the first Holocaust Remembrance Day program was extremely successful. We were in a small theater at the college. There were probably no more than forty people in the audience—a far cry from later Yom Hashoah commemorations! I sat on the stage and listened to myself being introduced. After explaining my reason for being there, I went into my story extemporaneously. I spoke for approximately

forty-five minutes, and there was absolute quiet and atten-
tiveness. I could feel a vibration drawing the audience and me
together. Later they came up tentatively to ask questions and
to look at the tattooed numbers on my arm. I was told later that
I had narrated my story in a powerful and moving way, and
that I had deeply affected the audience. Because of the sparse-
ness of the audience at this first gathering, I was asked to speak
again the following year.

In the meantime, something wonderful happened. Through
the hard work and commitment of Dean McCoy, Dr. Kaufman, and Dr. Charles Irace, who was then president of Raritan
Valley Community College, and later of the new president,
Dr. Cary Israel, and Dr. Tulsi Maharjan, and through my own
efforts and the efforts of other people at both the academic
and community levels, we developed a three-day workshop for
middle and high school students on the Holocaust and genocide. In addition, we established a writing contest, seminars for
teachers, and other special projects for the local community
related to the Holocaust and genocide. The Jewish Federation
of Somerset, Warren, and Hunterdon Counties, the New Jersey Holocaust Commission, and Raritan Valley Community
College support the program.

I am very committed to this program and serve on the
advisory panel. It is the only program of its kind in New Jersey.
We cannot accommodate all of the students who constitute
the audience for our program, so there is also a traveling exhibit.
We go out in groups to make our presentations throughout
New Jersey. Since the beginning of the program we have served
over fifty thousand students.

A recent incident at the end of a speaking engagement at
a charter school in New Brunswick moved me deeply. The students, mostly African American, sat in rapt attention as I told
my story. Afterward there were many questions; many of the

students were tearful during and after my presentation. At the very end, as I was packing my materials, a teacher, conspicuously pregnant, approached me. She identified herself as Leah and told me she was Jewish. In Jewish law, a child is usually named for a deceased close relative. So moved was she that she vowed to name her child, whether male or female, after one of my relatives murdered in the Holocaust. Never has an incident at one of my school presentations so moved me. And we pledged to stay in touch with one another, so that her promise to me might be fulfilled.

Something that puzzles our students deeply at the present time, as it does me, is denial of the Holocaust. We hear diatribes from racists, so-called skinheads, people who call themselves academicians, and sophisticated anti-Semites from around the world, who use not only print media but also the most advanced technology, in order to twist or negate the facts to which I and others were witnesses. All of them offer variations on the same theme: there was no Holocaust; there were no gas chambers, no six million men, women, and children murdered by the most diabolical means known to man. To all of them I pose the same questions: "If the Holocaust didn't happen, where are my father and mother, my dear relatives, and other people I knew who never came back? Can you explain to me where they are, and why I never saw them again?" I find it strange, even humorous in bizarre way, that the most efficient perpetrators of genocide in the world, and the best keepers of records of their crimes, have not been able to convince the deniers and revisionists that these horrors happened. Or is it that they have another agenda?

Because of the success of this ongoing program, its supporters undertook, beginning in 1995, with the help of the Jewish Federation and the leadership of Leonard Winters, chairperson of the Holocaust Advisory Committee, the establishment of the Raritan Valley Institute for Holocaust and Genocide Studies. I had had the vision, since my early involvement with the college, of establishing this resource center as a permanent community institution. In addition to the assistance of the Jewish Federation of Somerset, Warren, and Hunterdon Counties, it receives support from the New Jersey Department of Education and more than fifteen individuals who are donating their expertise and time as participants in and advisors to the institute's activities. Its dedication was planned for November 11, 1998, the sixtieth anniversary of the infamous desecration and burning of Jewish possessions and institutions throughout Germany and Austria known as Kristallnacht (Night of Broken Glass). However, because of unforeseen delays it was dedicated on April 18, 1999. The institute houses books, tapes, artifacts, and computers donated by people from our communities, all attesting to the vitality, the spirit, and the learning that could not be obliterated.

The mission of the Institute for Holocaust and Genocide Studies will be to make people aware of the causes and consequences of ethnic, racial, and religious intolerance; the actions necessary to prevent and curtail genocide; and the good deeds done by individuals during times of genocide. The institute will carry out its mission through a series of programs for the general community, particularly middle school and high school students. The programs will present to the students first-hand knowledge from survivors and experts on the Holocaust, genocide, ways to combat bigotry, and related subjects. In addition, the institute will concentrate intensely on training teachers to teach about the Holocaust, genocide, and prejudice reduction.

College-level courses have already been established at Raritan Valley Community College on these issues; furthermore, specific space has been established within the library for resource

materials on the Holocaust, genocide, and prejudice for the use
of local schools and the community. Finally, a memorial space
will be established within the institute room in memory of
the victims of the Holocaust. None of this could have been
achieved without the determination and encouragement of
Dr. Cary Israel, former president of Raritan Valley Community College. The current president, Dr. G. Jeremiah Ryan, has
also been supportive of the Holocaust Center's activities.

In 1981 New Jersey Governor Thomas Kean established the
Governor's Advisory Council on the Holocaust, which encour-
aged the development of Holocaust-genocide education. The
council was impressed with Raritan Valley's program and,
together with the Jewish Federation of Somerset, Warren, and
Hunterdon Counties, provided funds to promote the continuation and expansion of the program of teaching students in
local middle schools and high schools about the Holocaust.

I have been grateful for the opportunity to serve both on
the Advisory Council and later with the New Jersey Commission on Holocaust Education at the time of its inception. I
served under four governors: Thomas Kean, Jim Florio,
Christine Todd Whitman, and the present governor, James E.
McGreevey. In 1994 I testified before the State Legislature
about the importance of a mandatory statewide Holocaust
curriculum. I helped to spearhead a bill mandating statewide
education on the Holocaust for all grades, and have worked
with educators in planning the curriculum at every level.

At the same time, I continue to speak each academic year
to between forty and fifty schools. It is my hope that I have left
behind a message that one person can make a difference. I lived
through the deadly silence of the free world. I know the men-
acing power of evil, but I am equally acquainted with the more
dangerous, because more insidious, power of apathy. I remember

all the hours I spent in suffering, in anguish, and in physical and mental captivity, wondering not only about my personal fate, but also about why the world was silent. I wondered, "Where were the voices of decency, of democracy, of justice? Were they nowhere to be found? Had they been found, could not even a few of the sixty-eight members of my family who had perished been saved?" But my suffering had left me determined to dedicate whatever time had been allotted to me to teach and to raise questions, so that fewer and fewer oppressed persons and victims of tyranny and bigotry would feel the abandonment my people and I had felt in the Holocaust.

CHAPTER
## 12

# Revisiting the Past

In July 1995 Harvey and I took a tour of Scandinavia. My main reason for going on this trip was to return to Sweden in order to see the country that had given me back my life after the Holocaust, and to express my gratitude in some way to the country that had sheltered and fed and restored other survivors and myself, disabled and ill as we had been. To backtrack a bit, when Harvey and I married I told him the story of how much Sweden and its people meant to me. He made a commitment then to take me back there someday, so that both of us could give thanks for what that nation had bestowed on us.

Here is a portion of the letter sent to me by Marna Feldt, the information officer of the Swedish Consulate in New York on July 5, 1995, telling me that arrangements had been made for us to visit the new Judiska Museeti (Jewish Museum) in Stockholm on July 17:

> The Curator of the Museum, Paula Gringer, will receive you. Mrs. Gringer was saved in the famous boat evacuation across the Sound from Denmark to Sweden in October 1943, just before the Nazi occupation forces in Denmark began to round up all the Danish Jews. . . . You indicated you wanted to give

a "reward" of some sort. We believe that the Jewish Museum would be a most appropriate recipient, if you so wish. Mrs. Gringer will be honored to receive you, and to guide you around the Museum and the special exhibition now on display commemorating the 50th year after the Holocaust.

The "reward" mentioned in the letter referred to a plaque that I took with me to present to the museum. This plaque expressed my personal gratitude for the metamorphosis in my life for which my year's residence in Sweden had been responsible, but I wanted it to speak for others as well. (A replica of this plaque appears in the photo gallery that is part of this book.)

Driving from the airport to Stockholm once Harvey and I had arrived in Sweden, I tried to visualize and recreate the past for myself. I wanted to recreate the parks and streets and buildings of the time when I had lived there, but it was impossible for me to do so. Still, I was gratified to be able to return to the place where I had been saved.

On our first day in Stockholm we visited the Jewish Museum. As promised, Paula Gringer and her assistant met us there. Paula gratefully accepted the plaque I had taken and another gift, a medal that had been presented to me by the New Jersey Commission for Holocaust Education. The only question was where to display them. Harvey and I looked at one another, and we realized that both the plaque and the medal should rest in the Jewish Museum in Stockholm. They are presently mounted on a prominent wall. I am pleased to say that there are also documents about me and a picture of me there.

My only regret during my visit to Stockholm was that I missed seeing a wonderful ninety-year-old lady who was on vacation. She had been in charge of welcoming me and my

fellow Holocaust survivors to Sweden fifty years earlier. However, we were to have our own separate reunion on April 15,
1996, when she came to New York to give a program at the
Ninety-second Street YMCA.

One highlight of my journey to Sweden was a trip on a
ferry that runs regularly between Sweden and Denmark. It is
only a half-hour trip, but I wanted desperately to have the
ferry follow the exact route that the Danish and Norwegian
Jews had traveled in their flight from the Nazis and the Holocaust. Could the group director arrange this, I wondered. He
explained our desires to the ferry people, and they agreed to
accommodate us. Retracing that brief but memorable and poignant journey, I recited many prayers and shed many tears.

While in Copenhagen, we sought out many Danish-Jewish
survivors to find out what had actually happened there during
the Nazi occupation. We were told that the Danish King,
Christian X, had never actually marched down the street wearing a yellow Star of David armband. That had been a fable. But
he did say to the Nazis, "These are my people. They are Danes,
and you are not going to harm them!" For this act of defiance
and for aiding the escape of the Danish Jews to Sweden, the
king was held under house arrest for two years.

We had missed seeing the synagogue in Stockholm, so our
first request to the guide in Copenhagen was to visit the one
there. He agreed, and the bus dropped us off near the temple.
Tall wrought-iron gates protected the building. It displayed no
Jewish star, and there was no Hebrew visible anywhere. We were
able to identify the building as a synagogue only because it had
the twelve traditional windows, one for each of the twelve
tribes.

We rang the bell for a very long time before a lady responded
from within. We identified ourselves as Jews from the United
States and said that we would like to go in and make a donation.

She refused to open the doors. We spoke to her in Yiddish, and she said she was sorry, but since we did not have official clearance papers, she could not let us in.

Disappointed and a little shocked, we retreated. Two days later, Harvey read in *USA Today* that there had been a bomb threat to the synagogue, the Jewish cemetery, and the Israeli Embassy. I was sick over the whole experience, but those living there are accustomed to terrorist threats. It was ironic to us that the country that had saved so many Jews, with so many good ordinary citizens participating at risk to their own lives, should now be besieged by fear of terrorism. Danish Jews, living in a proud bastion of democracy, were walking in fear. They were unable to enter their synagogues when they wanted to, and security police had to be stationed outside during the high holy days. Even more demeaning, the worshippers were required to present ID cards before entering the synagogue. One man wearing a yarmulke told me, "We can practice our Judaism, but not freely. They really don't like us."

The best jewelry store in Copenhagen is owned by a Holocaust survivor. The store is a local landmark because in the window there is a little toy train bedecked with diamonds and other jewels making a circuit around a track. As we entered, the merchant greeted us warmly. Suddenly he spotted the numbers on my arm, and his smile froze. Just as suddenly, he began to shed tears. He had lost his entire family in the camps. He pleaded with me to pick out anything I wanted in the store, but I thanked him and shook my head. In conversation, he told us that many survivors had settled in Denmark after the war. These survivors lecture in the schools and serve as bearers of witness, and the Holocaust is part of the school curriculum of the country.

From Denmark we made a brief trip to Norway. Norway is the most picturesque country I have ever seen. Our tour guide walked us in the footsteps of those Norwegian heroes who fought fiercely against the Third Reich. We saw the barracks, gun emplacements, bunkers, and even parade grounds. It was made abundantly clear to us that the memories of the German occupation and German atrocities are still vivid and horrifying to those Norwegians who lived through the Second World War.

On April 30, 1996, we made a return trip to Hungary. This time our friends Susan and Sheldon Guss and Maxwell and Carolyn Borow accompanied us. Sheldon and Maxwell were attending a medical convention in Budapest. This journey was completely different in nature from the one in 1972. That journey had been personal and familial, with several purposes: to visit my grandfathers' graves, to be reunited with my uncle Henrik, to acquaint my children with the world from which I had arisen, and to bring together three generations whose lives had been irrevocably altered by the Holocaust.

This time, however, our journey was more specific and businesslike. My uncle was no longer alive, and every emotional tie with the land of my birth had been severed. The Eastern European countries were beginning to make reparations to the surviving victims of the Holocaust whose homes and property had been confiscated. As a claimant, I had filed papers with the federal government of Hungary.

In late January or early February 1996 I was informed that my case was coming up for a hearing within a month (at the end of February). I immediately took matters into my own hands. I wrote to the Hungarian court, informing them that I would be in Hungary at the end of April and that I wanted to be present for the hearings on reparations. The court acknowledged my request, and I received a "court date" of May 3 to make arguments. We made arrangements to hire a Hungarian lawyer named Dr. Mesko Tomas.

The lawyer met me at my hotel. We went over my papers carefully and awaited the May 3 hearing date. The day finally came. We arrived at court. The building was a beautiful one from the outside, but what occurred inside wasn't nearly so beautiful. We were called not into the courtroom but into the private chambers of a lady judge, Dr. Horvath. Six of us were in the room: Harvey, my lawyer, the judge, a court official, a stenographer, and I.

The lawyer made his presentation. I was laying claim, he explained, to the house, the general store, and the parcels of land, including vineyards, that had belonged to my family. Once he presented my case, however, the judge asked me if I had a "deed" to the property that I was claiming. Shocked, I answered that since we had been taken forcibly and quickly from our homes, there was no way we could have had time to gather papers; nor would we have been able to keep them with us if we had done so. I recollected bitterly how willingly our former neighbors and friends had cooperated with our deportation, and how ready they had seemed to expropriate our property and possessions.

The judge expressed her sympathy. I then asked her why the original deed hadn't been searched out prior to my arrival, so that it would be ready for presentation at the hearing. The judge said she would postpone the proceedings until September in order to enable me to find the papers. I thanked her, although I was emotionally upset over the negligence of the Hungarian legal system to gather the materials that would provide evidence of my claim.

Outside the judge's chambers, our lawyer informed Harvey and me that a search would be very costly for us and without any guarantee that I would, in fact, eventually receive compensation. We walked out into the daylight realizing that this was the "closure" to my case. My life was in America. The final connection with Hungary had been cut. Neither family nor property existed for me in my native land.

Leaving the court area, we found our friends waiting for us downstairs. Susan's cousins Stefen and Susana Attar, who live in Budapest, had arranged for us a tour of the Herend china factory. It felt good for the moment to act like an ordinary tourist. Once again we had rented a car.

The next day we went to Tolscva for what I had determined would be a final visit. Our friends wanted to see my old home, and I wanted to see my maternal grandfather's grave one more time. This time we did not go to Horvaty, my father's village. There was no longer a Jewish cemetery there.

In Tolscva things were different from what they had been in 1972. Like the rest of Hungary, Tolscva was being "modernized." When we came to my street, my house was no longer there. It had been leveled. It was difficult for me to determine even where it had stood. We drove around the street, and finally I saw a familiar group of houses and could at last gauge the spot where my house had stood. Standing on the spot, I announced to my friends, "This was my home."

We entered one of the houses adjoining what I had determined was the site of my family's property. I spoke to the owner of the house. Suddenly her next-door neighbor came in. This turned out to be a woman named Huszak, the woman who, more than fifty years earlier, had come to our house each Sabbath morning to light our lights and to turn on our oven, since Orthodox Jews are forbidden to kindle a fire on the Sabbath. We hugged and kissed one another. She cried and sighed, telling me she remembered my family.

Then came a younger man whose family lived nearby. He, too, had tears. He hadn't even been born at the time we were taken away. His father had owned wine cellars, where people could rent space to store wines. My father had been a renter of his. The young man invited us to come with him on a visit to one of the cellars. We consented to accompany him, and Mrs. Huszak joined us.

As we walked up toward the end of the village, we came upon a house of a once prominent family who were said to have been descended from Hungarian nobility. The house looked rather dilapidated from the outside. The daughter of the house emerged from within, and Mrs. Huszak told her who I was. I did not recognize her. She had purple blotches on her face. She extended a hand, saying, "Muncika, look at you. You look so beautiful and young. You couldn't have suffered so much!"

I was shocked and chagrined beyond my power to comprehend or respond. How could this woman be so dismissive of what I had experienced? She kept on talking about her brother and sister. But I blocked the rest of her words completely out of my mind. Finally, I walked away.

Harvey and my friends saw immediately how upset I was. Susan put her arm around me and told me to forget about the incident; however, I still remember this brief encounter vividly, and the memory of the episode has a stinging effect.

The young man, too, perceived what had occurred. Hoping to help us forget and to restore a semblance of serenity to the tense atmosphere, he invited us to continue our journey to the wine cellar. When we got there Harvey, Maxwell, and Shelly went in, but I could not. Facing the wine cellar were lilac bushes that seemed to reach out to me. But I could not even touch them because they evoked the memory of my mother.

When the cellar tour was over, the young man emerged with a siphon full of wine and several small glasses. He gave each of us a glass of wine to taste. It was delicious. The taste took me back to the joyous days of my past. He then filled a Coca-Cola bottle with wine for each of us to take with us. The young man also made me a bouquet of flowers. We stayed for a while in the vineyards and looked around. Finally we said goodbye to the young man and to some of the neighbors who had followed us.

I directed the driver to go past the synagogue I had attended, which was on the main street of Tolcsva, where all the shops were as well. West of the main street, we found the school that I had attended. It looked exactly the same. We then directed the driver to take us to the Jewish cemetery. The front gate was no longer there, and it was overgrown. I was determined to get in, and I began to propel myself through the gigantic shrubbery. I could not find my grandfather's grave. My friends tried to help me pull out the tall weeds, but we simply could not get to the grave. The weeds were taller than we were. Stones were broken into fragments. In sadness and resignation we recited the mourner's Kaddish and left.

Before we had departed for Hungary, I had written to my aunt Boszke, informing her of our upcoming trip. I had received no reply from her. Susan had written a letter to her cousin informing him of my not having heard anything from my aunt. Then Susan's cousin Stefen wrote a letter to Sarospatak, the town where my aunt had lived. This letter was given by the postal service to a couple named Pasztor who had been close friends of my aunt and uncle. The Pasztors replied to Stefen in a letter, saying that Boszke had passed away in October 1995. They also enclosed their telephone number. I had immediately called them and made arrangements to meet with them when I got to Sarospatak.

After we left Tolscva we drove to Sarospatak and went to the home of the Pasztors. All of us had lunch in the restaurant at the town's hotel. At lunch I primarily conversed in Hungarian with the Pasztors. They brought me up to date about Boszke's last years. What puzzled me most was why Boszke had not been buried alongside my uncle Henrik. Since he had died in the hospital in Satoraljeujhely, the Orthodox Jewish burial society there had taken it upon themselves to bury him within the twenty-four hour period ordained by Jewish law. They would not take the time to transport his body to Sarospatak. I was told that Bozske had felt very bitter and upset at the burial society's usurpation of the funeral arrangements. After Henrik's death, I was told, she had become very melancholy and ill and had simply lost her desire to live. Bozske is buried in Sarospatak near her immediate family.

After lunch we followed Mr. Pazstor to Satoraljaujhely, where my uncle Henrik is buried. On the outskirts of the town is a well-tended, gated Jewish cemetery. At he entrance we saw a beautiful building, the purpose of which we never learned. The Jewish caretaker told us that this was the cemetery where the greatest *tzadikim* (the most learned and pious rabbis) of the Zemplen Megye region were buried.

We followed the caretaker, who guided us with his car to the cemetery where Henrik is buried. His grave is atop a hill. When I found his tombstone I went to it immediately, embraced it, and had a little "talk" with him. I found on the tombstone the names of his two young daughters, Edith and Erzsike, who had died with their mother in Auschwitz. He had probably left instructions with Bozske to have their names added in the event that his death preceded hers. I must add that I was happy with his tombstone, the only truly whole one in my family. In 1974, a year after his death, we had sent money to Bozske to make sure a proper monument would be placed over his grave.

After we spent some time at the grave and said *Kaddish*, we left the cemetery and followed Mr. Pasztor back to Sarospatak. He took us to his apartment, and his wife served us refreshments. I asked them if they had taken any family heirlooms from my aunt and uncle's apartment that I might give to my aunt Minnie on my return to the United States. Mrs. Pasztor gave me some the possessions and all the pictures that we had sent to my uncle and aunt from America.

Once we had concluded our visit, we departed for Budapest. On our trip back to the city I sat quietly with the driver in the van we had rented. All sorts of memories were milling through my mind, but I felt an inner peace because I had been there to pay my last visit to those who had been dear to me. But I was also haunted by the realization that all I had left of my family in Hungary was a few graves.

In Budapest we had wanted to visit the Dohany Synagogue on the Sabbath, but it was still being renovated, so we could not enter it. However, we went to a service around the corner. The service was held in a small synagogue annex used for that purpose. On the street we saw an Orthodox Jew dressed in traditional black garb, walking to Sabbath services. I was heartened to see any sign of a resurgence of Judaism in Hungary.

We saw the memorial tree with its silver leaves containing the names of the Hungarian Jews who had perished in the Holocaust. Since it was the Sabbath, the gates were closed for fear of vandalism. During the weekdays there are guards stationed at the gates to prevent vandals from getting in. This disturbed me; it was 1996, and Jewish property, as well as Jews themselves, was still not immune to harm. Had the world learned anything?

We decided to visit an open-air flea market. On the way there, we were nearly mugged by several thugs. Thankfully, Harvey and Sheldon Guss pushed us out of harm's way and chased our would-be assailants, as I yelled a few well-chosen and not very genteel Hungarian phrases at them. Thus we were able to continue on our way.

At the bazaar, while we were inspecting some hand-embroidered merchandise and children's toys, we met a middle-aged man of the Second Generation who owned one of the booths. We bought some things from him, mostly because we had sympathy for his present situation. Both of his elderly parents had survived the Holocaust, but they did not want to leave Hungary despite all they had suffered in their native country. He had chosen to remain with them, even though there was little future for him there.

There was one more significant encounter in Budapest. I had met and become friends with a woman named Marica Lane in Somerville, New Jersey, many years earlier. Now she was visiting her mother, Mrs. Vargananie, in Budapest at the same time we were there. Marica's father had died in the Holocaust, but Marica and her mother had stayed alive because they had hidden in cellars and attics and other places, living on potato peelings and whatever else they could find. Marica later married Michael Lane, another Holocaust survivor, and she owns a dress shop in Somerville. Each year her mother had come to visit her in the United States. The meeting in Budapest was the last I had with her mother, since she died a little over a year later.

From Hungary we went on a bus to Vienna. I was very uncomfortable hearing the German language constantly in Vienna, and had it not been for the group with whom I was traveling, I would not have gone there. However, something very pleasant occurred there. Susan and Shelly Guss had had an Austrian exchange student named Michael Lang living with them in the United States. He and his family live in Vienna. The young man met us in our hotel upon our arrival in Vienna. He took us on a tour of the central part of the city so that we would get our bearings. We had two delightful and delicious dinners, one at his home and one at his wife's parents' home, and we met the rest of his family.

When Michael's father-in-law saw the numbers tattooed on my arm, his mood saddened. "I must apologize to you," he said with deep sincerity, "for the loss of your family and for what the Jewish people had endured during the Holocaust." I am certain that, as an Austrian, he felt deep sorrow to have to regard Hitler as his compatriot. "Would that more of his countrymen felt the same," I thought.

On another occasion during our stay, Maxwell Borow's cousin, David Borow, who had gone to medical school in Vienna and is a physician there, contacted us. He visited with us, and he and his wife accompanied us on several excursions through the city. They were able to arrange for us, with considerable difficulty, to visit the synagogue in Vienna. This synagogue had not been destroyed during the Kristallnacht pogrom of 1938 and had never been touched during the war years. However, when we arrived there we found that we could not go into the main sanctuary; the doors were padlocked, and numerous security guards surrounded the building. We were searched for anything suspicious that we might have been carrying.

Witnessing this scene, I felt contradictory emotions. Why, I asked myself, was it necessary so many years after the Holocaust for Jews to have to endure the uncertainty and terror of destructive acts against us from people who continued to hate us after everything we had endured? On the other hand, there was a certain feeling of assurance that at least the government was taking some measures to protect Jewish institutions from violence and destruction. If only such actions as the securing of synagogues and the protection of Jewish life in general had taken place decades earlier!

One more incident during the Vienna portion of our trip is worthy of note. One day our group had gone out to lunch. I had my wallet with me, which contained some American dollars, as well as cards and papers of identification. At one point after we had returned to the hotel, I reached for my wallet and found it was not there. I reported the missing wallet to the concierge of the hotel. He told me to retrace my steps, returning to the various places we had been.

We immediately called a cab and returned to the central part of the city, going from place to place and inquiring whether anyone had turned in the wallet. We were told to go to the police station in the district where I had lost it. Upon entering the police station, I was asked to identify myself and state my purpose in being there. After I had given them my name and shown them identification, they asked me to come in. Immediately I was told that they had found my wallet. The officer in charge came in with the wallet, holding in his hand the ID card indicating that I am a member of the New Jersey Commission on Holocaust Education. They asked me what the card represented. I'm not certain whether they were struck by the word *Holocaust* or whether they thought I was a person of some official status. In any event, they became very respectful and solicitous of my welfare. They told me that they couldn't return the cash, because it was being held as evidence (the pickpocket whom they had caught had stolen many wallets that day). However, I was reassured that the Austrian government would return my stolen money to me. I told them that for their kindness I wanted to donate the money to the children of members of their Policeman's Benevolent Association.

It was the last day of our trip. We could happily tell our friends that my wallet had been found. I was happy for another reason. I felt somehow as though my physical journey into my European past had finally come to an end and that I had brought as much closure to the past as I was able to. I thought

I could now focus on my family of today and on my educational mission of translating the pain of the past for the generations of the future, so that they might learn from it. A day later we returned to the United States to await the birth of our first grandson, Joshua.

CHAPTER

# 13

# *Lest We Forget*

God has blessed me with three grandchildren: Caryn, the daughter of Tina, and Joshua and Zachary, the sons of Joseph. Joshua was born on May 24, 1996, and Zachary, the most recent arrival, was born on September 19, 1998.

Caryn is the light of my life. As I mentioned earlier, she was born the same day that Philip, Aunt Minnie's oldest son, died. My joy on the day of her birth was mingled with grief at the death of my cousin, but at least one life was given for the one taken away. I was reminded once again, in a very personal way, that the life cycle continues and that joy and sorrow are often intermingled.

Caryn reminds me very much of Tina as a little girl. When Caryn was very small and I used to bathe her, she would notice the numbers on my arm. In speaking to adults I often refer to them as "Hitler's footsteps on my body." However, I was perplexed as to what I might say to her. I was conscious that the numbers disturbed her. She referred to them as "bubu," and she wanted to wash them off with a washcloth. Finally, when she was old enough, I told her that "a bad man did this to 'Mama' [which is what she still calls me]." She has now grown into a beautiful, studious, and caring young lady. I am very proud of her accomplishments, but even more of her sensitivity and kindness.

Joshua is lovable and affectionate and tends to wear his emotions on his sleeve. Like his father, he is a complete extrovert. At the age of two he is also affected by my arm with its numbers; he wants to pull the numbers out. He is very articulate, with a wonderful vocabulary, and he has the ability to gauge my feelings. He knows when I am upset and when I feel sad, and responds with "Grandma Margit, are you OK?" He comes to me with hugs and kisses, and nothing feels more wonderful to me than that.

Zachary is just as lovable and affectionate, but he is also determined to find his place in the family constellation, as are so many second children. Whenever I visit, he makes certain that he is the first to hug and kiss me.

My grandchildren provide me with joy, but I am also troubled that all three are affected by having a grandmother who is a Holocaust survivor.

Two events of recent years stand out in my mind because they brought home to me the idea that we must link the past to the present. Both events occurred in my community. The first took place at Congregation Knesset Israel in Bound Brook on the morning of November 16, 1986. At that time my family and I dedicated a Holocaust Torah in loving memory of the Buchhalter and Granat families. Rabbi Aaron Deckter, the spiritual leader of Knesset Israel, was instrumental in helping us acquire this very special Torah. Bill Rosenberg, our attorney, who is also a dear friend and fellow congregant, handled all the legal paperwork for both obtaining the Torah and transferring it to us. Without his efforts we could not have accomplished our mission, and I am deeply grateful to him.

A *Torah* is a scroll of parchment on which is written the first five books of the Bible, the books of Moses. It is produced by a scribe using a special kind of ink and pen. It is rolled up and stored in a cover, and the handles used to unfurl the scroll are adorned with crowns. The Torah has a breastplate, a decoration that enhances its appearance. A Torah is housed in a sacred ark known as an *a'haron kodesh*.

The Torah we acquired was the Sefer Torah. It had survived the destruction that had taken place in the now extinct Jewish community of Libochovice, Czechoslovakia. Like countless other Jewish symbols, it had been confiscated by the Nazis and shipped to a depository in Prague, where it lain waiting to be displayed in Hitler's intended "museum" depicting what he hoped to be the remnants of the "extinct Jewish race." Some two decades after the war, this Torah, along with other artifacts, was released to the Westminster Synagogue in London and reposed there.

We needed a Torah mantle and *gartel* (the belt that holds the Torah scroll together) and the other accessories necessary to a Torah service. One day in August of that year I went with Eleanor Borow and Susan Guss to Miriam's Religious Objects, a store on Canal Street on the Lower East Side of Manhattan. There a memorable encounter took place.

I wanted the Torah accoutrements to reflect the theme of the Holocaust. To my great amazement, I discovered that the owner of the store, Miriam, was herself a survivor from Hungary. I had heard her speak in Hungarian and started to talk with her in our native language. I asked her where she was from, and she told me. Then I noticed the numbers on her arm. She said she had been in Auschwitz. While comparing our numbers we both realized that she had been only twenty-nine people ahead of me in line. We had therefore both arrived on the same

day. Since I hadn't received my numbers until my return to
Auschwitz, this meant she had also been with me in Cracow!

She reminded me of an incident in which she had been
involved in Cracow. Miriam had been trying to help a pregnant girl who was unable to lift a heavy stone. The girl had
received a brutal beating and lost her baby. Miriam is still blam-
ing herself today for that loss.

During our unexpected reunion Miriam and I embraced and
cried. My friends tried to comfort us; at the same time they, too,
had tears in their eyes. The incident proved to me, once again,
that a survivor might relive the Holocaust at any moment,
since none of us ever knows when we will encounter a fellow
survivor or any other person or event that awakens memories
of that past life.

Miriam was a remarkable designer, and she designed this
Torah cover in a unique way. She used materials of different
colors to depict flames rising into the heavens representing the
burning of our people. Brown, gold, and orange "flames" reach
upward against a white background. (Photos of the Torah cover
and other accoutrements appear in the photo gallery that is part
of this book.)

A metals craftsman named Stanley Miller from Fleming-
ton, New Jersey, made the Torah crowns and breastplate and
the pointer. The two crowns resemble the barbed wire fences
surrounding the camps, from which bodies and arms reach up
to the skies. The breastplate resembles the burning bush of the
book of Exodus in the Bible.

This Sefer Torah is especially meaningful to me now, as I
know that our perished brethren used it and many young boys
studied from it for their bar mitzvot and afterward. The Torah
always played an important part in the life of Eastern European
Jews. Because the Torah was not brought here merely for

ornamental purposes, but to be used by the Bound Brook congregation, it provides a vital link between the past and the future. All who study from it and read from it will be reminded automatically of the Holocaust and of the generations that were its victims.

In the ceremony held was to formally present the Sefer Torah to the congregation, my role was to present the Torah and to thank everyone involved for making the day possible. In my speech I charged my children with the responsibility of caring for the Torah and discharging its mission. I felt both inner peace and parental pride knowing how much caring for this Torah meant to them. I also expressed in my speech my sadness that, while the name of Granat will continue because my uncles who came here in the early twentieth century had male offspring to carry on the name, the name of Buchhalter will not be carried on because all who bore it have perished.

I must confess that, since I live in Bridgewater and my granddaughter, Caryn, goes to Hebrew School at Temple Shalom, Harvey and I wanted to worship there with our family. We joined that temple and about two years ago had the Sefer Torah transferred there. It took almost a year to acquire permission and release from Westminster Synagogue. Each time I am in temple I am reassured because Rabbi Isaacs makes constant use of it ceremonially.

Sunday, April 9, 1995, was one of the most memorable nights of my life. Along with others, I had long before made a commitment to speak and teach about and remember the Holocaust. But in 1995 our communities took a major step to enhance that possibility for even more people by undertaking the establishment of the Holocaust and Genocide Studies Institute at Raritan Valley Community College. April 9 was the night of a gala fund-raiser to provide the financial foundation for this vision.

The guest speaker was Holocaust survivor and author Elie Wiesel, and I was the honoree.

That night we were also observing the fiftieth anniversary of the liberation of the concentration camps. For me this was a reminder of all I had suffered during the terrible months in Auschwitz, Cracow, Grunberg, and Bergen-Belsen and of the gratitude I could now feel not only for having lived past those horrors, but for being afforded the opportunity to ponder in awe the miracle of transformation within my own life.

I could still remember myself as the starved and frightened girl of fifteen in concentration camp garb, her hair shorn, her appearance indistinguishable from that of other prisoners, her life worth nothing to her persecutors, who could easily have destroyed it on a whim with a bullet, a rope, or even a fist. But I also saw myself as I was that night, amid friends and loved ones who had come to honor me and to support my own vision of creating a place and an opportunity for education so that the young *and* their elders would be aware of the terrible consequences of hatred, bigotry, and persecution.

Approximately one thousand people attended the gala on April 9. There were greetings and remarks by Leonard Knauer, president of the Jewish Federation of Somerset, Hunterdon, and Warren Counties; Dr. Cary Israel, president of Raritan Valley Community College; Senator James McGreevey of the Nineteenth District; Assemblyman Christopher Bateman of the Sixteenth District; Congressman Richard Zimmer of the Twelfth District; Fred Howlett of the Somerset County Board of Freeholders; James Dowden, mayor of Bridgewater; Maury Laulicht, chairman of the New Jersey Commission on Holocaust Education; and Sister Rose Thering of Seton Hall University and the Holocaust Commission.

In his keynote address Elie Wiesel implored the audience not to forget the Holocaust. "The human mind is such that it cannot retain everything," he said. "What will happen to the faces we [the survivors] have seen, the children we have forgotten?" Responding to the frequently uttered charge that we Jews speak too much about our suffering, he said that what matters is "what we do with our suffering." He continued, "We invoke memories to reduce suffering for everyone. We speak of our past because we don't want our past to become part of our children's future." He talked of his fear that the Holocaust will become trivialized. "I want the subject to remain sacred," he told us. "I admire everyone who teaches it. It is the most important subject to teach."

Wiesel told of the horrors perpetrated in the death camps and on the marches, and of his father, who had been with him during his terrible days in Auschwitz, providing him with the will to remain alive so long as they were not separated from one another. He recounted the death of his father, who had been his pillar of strength, and his own subsequent despair as a result of his loss. He told of his liberation and of the gratitude of the survivors when in April 1945 the American soldiers finally arrived to liberate them. Describing the thankfulness of the survivors in the moments when they realized that rescue was at hand, he observed, "When the liberators came, some children were so weak that when they applauded they were not at all applauding. They did not have the strength to."

Before the program had gotten under way, several protestors began a demonstration at the front entrance to the college theater. They carried signs with crude and cruel messages denying the Holocaust, mocking Jewish claims, and referring to Elie Wiesel as a "notorious prevaricator." In Wiesel's speech he referred to the demonstrators, saying, "I would never grant them the dignity of a debate. Let them be devoured by their own hatred." Sad as was the spectacle of Holocaust denial and anti-Semitism, it brought home to us all the more clearly the great need for education at all levels about the horrors that Elie Wiesel and I and countless others had lived through.

Before Elie Wiesel spoke I was called to the stage, along with Wiesel and Stephen Offen, the incoming president of the federation. I was presented with a magnificent gift that I will always treasure: a sculpture by Marian Slepian called *Margit's Journey*. (A photo of this sculpture appears on the back flap of the jacket of this book.) Marian, a resident of Bridgewater, was the presenter. She is an artist of national renown. In creating this work, she used an ancient technique called cloisonné, in which enamel is applied to metal in cells delineated by soldered wires and then fired. The full effect of this work is both emotional in its tone and visually stunning in its fusion of line and color.

The sculpture is divided into four sections. In the lowest section is depicted a world of evil in which a serpent destroys by fire the civilized world (represented by broken rocks and crumbling buildings), innocence and peace (a dove), and the Jewish people (the Star of David). As the viewer's eye moves up to the next section, though, it sees that the burning bush is not consumed, as the Jewish people are not consumed, but rises from the ashes. In the second section, to the right is an inset that depicts Jerusalem reborn. To the left is a series of squares and circles depicting wholeness and completion.

The third section shows Jacob's ladder, symbolizing survival and return to life. Above and directly to the left of the ladder is a fish, a Biblical symbol of redemption. The open eye of the fish represents the eye of God, ever watchful, never sleeping. Between the two upper sections is the sea: the passage from captivity to freedom. In the uppermost section we find a sacrificial ram, representing the redemption of Isaac; a branch of a hewn tree, symbolizing the surviving remnant of the Holocaust; the Eternal Light; the Star of David; and a rainbow symbolizing the covenant between God and the Jewish people. Running through the sections like a visual leitmotif are the words (in Hebrew lettering) *Ayshet Chayil* (Woman of Valor). The sculpture depicts the struggle of the Jewish people through history, but also my struggle through the Holocaust.

When I was asked to speak, I called Marian Slepian to the stage to acknowledge her and thank her for the love she had put into the creation of this work of art. I thanked the audience for the masterpiece they had presented to me. I asked all of the survivors and the members of the Second and Third Generations to rise and symbolically accept the work in honor of the survivors and in memory of those who had perished. "As long as I live," I said, "I shall cherish this evening and this gift."

I went on to welcome and to thank the varied groups who had come to honor me. I thanked them for their kindness to me personally over the years and for their willingness to support Holocaust and genocide education. I addressed Elie Wiesel in particular, acknowledging him as "my mentor and a *zaddik* [spiritual leader] of my heritage." I thanked God for Wiesel's survival, since "no one can tell the world our pain, our sufferings, and our hopes as you can." And I quoted his words: "Fifty years ago, we survivors awoke and found ourselves orphans in an orphaned world."

I marveled at the fact that, given what had happened to me fifty years earlier, I could be standing before an audience of a thousand people, being honored. I said, "Fifty-one years ago, when I was a fourteen-year-old child, my world went up in flames, and the free world was silent. I was taken from my home with my family and put in a ghetto where we awaited our deportation to Auschwitz-Birkenau Concentration Camp. It was there that I saw for the last time my beloved parents, grandmothers, aunts, uncles, and cousins, whose faces, voices, and love will remain with me forever."

I told of the incident of my father's stepping out of line and blessing me before he was savagely attacked and taken from me forever. I spoke of the camps I was in and of Anne Frank, who had been with me in Bergen-Belsen and perished just a month before we were liberated. I reflected on the meaning of my birthday, which is both a celebration and a day of remembrance for me, for it is on my birthday that I say Kaddish for Anne Frank.

I went on to express my gratitude to the United States and to the state of New Jersey, which offered me thousands of other survivors the setting and the freedom in which to rebuild our lives, in return for which "we offer our memories and our commitment that this will never happen again."

I thanked my husband, Harvey, and my children, Tina and Joseph, for their love and understanding, and referred to "my beautiful, precious granddaughter, Caryn, in whom I see the continuation of my family." (At that time, my grandsons were not yet born, but I am certain that they will provide two other precious links in the chain of my ongoing family.)

I pledged to dedicate my life to further educating others about the consequences of inhumanity and to keep alive the memory of those who had perished. Finally, I challenged those in the audience who have power and influence "to go forward from this place" and create a model of education for the entire United States, so that people might "learn to love and respect one another, and always stand up and speak when any injustice occurs."

I concluded with these words: "I look upon tonight as a new beginning on my continuing journey, and hope that you will help me turn my dream of a permanent Holocaust and

Genocide Institute at Raritan Valley Community College into
a reality."

That dream was realized at the dedication of the Holocaust
Genocide Institute on April 18, 1999.

I often think of the meaning of the cloisonné artwork that was
given to me on that glorious spring night in 1995, which now
graces my home. I marvel at the way in which Marian Slepian
captured both individual and collective history. Sadly but
surely, my life is not unique: all too many suffered what I did
and did not survive. I have been among the remnant that has
made the journey from suffering, dislocation, and anguish to
redemption, stability, and renewal. In the end, the serpent did
not destroy me, nor did the fire consume me. I found a branch
of the tree that had been cut and clung to it. I cannot know for
certain whether the ever-open eye of God was upon me when
the day of liberation came, but I continue to believe in God's
covenant with me and my people, even though my fate was
sorely tested in the Holocaust.

Have I earned the title Woman of Valor? I do not know. I
do know that during the time I spent in hell my main objec-
tive was not to show courage, or defiance, or extraordinary
godliness. It was simply to stay alive another day, another hour,
to get the next ration of food, to see another dawn. Many far
braver than I perished. I survived through neither cunning
nor courage; perhaps I survived only through blind luck.

Much was taken from me; much was also restored. But I
must believe that I have a purpose: to bear witness, and to bear
to others, particularly the young, a knowledge of the depths
of evil I have seen so that they will know this evil exists, and
that we can prevent it only when we do not turn our heads
away from it. This is my commitment, and this is my continuing journey.

# TESTIMONIES AND LETTERS
## FROM FAMILY MEMBERS

# Harvey Feldman

In the early days of our life together, Margit used to tell me of her experiences and those of her family when she was thirteen or fourteen years old. I could not understand how anybody could have survived those conditions. She told me also about Sweden, how her life had been saved there, and I promised her that when the right time came we would go back and thank those people, which we did. We also made two trips to Hungary.

My wife must be very, very strong. When she speaks to students and teachers at middle schools, high schools, colleges, and universities, I can no longer sit in the room and listen to her experiences. It's too painful. I did not lose my family in the Holocaust, but after I heard her story I felt as though *I* had lost all the Jews: as if every Jew—man, woman, and child—was part of my family. They perished in an era that I will never understand.

When I was ten or eleven years old, living in Brooklyn, I remember picking up the newspapers every day to read about what was going on in Europe. There wasn't too much media communication—no TV at all, just a little on the radio. When I told Margit about this, her response was, "How could you know?" When we went to the U.S. Holocaust Museum in

Washington, D.C., I pointed to the newspapers on the wall of the exhibit, the very articles I had read in the *New York Times*, the *Daily News*, the *Journal-American*, and the *New York Post*. "That's how I knew!" I said.

The fact is, however, that the past did not really come into the present for me until my wife became involved with Jewish organizations. Only a person who had gone through what she went through could be so committed. I'm amazed, for example, that she never holds a grudge. She has to ask people to contribute money for the state of Israel. Some of them have hung up on her, and some won't even speak to her because she asks them for money. But she doesn't take it personally; she goes on giving of herself, because she knows what it means to have and to support a Jewish state. Who can possibly know better than she?

# B

## Tina Feldman

Through the entire fabric of my life my mother's strength has been woven. She is my rock and my savior. She taught me to appreciate the simple pleasures of life, like her wonderful Hungarian cooking, or the love of beautiful flowers. She has given me a feeling for high moral standards and ethics. She has been a mentor to many others as well. She is committed to her family, but she can also appreciate the worth of every human being. She has never forgotten to care for "Grandma Boehm" (her Aunt Minnie), who cared for her when she first came to this country. She has never refused to help my daughter Caryn or me when we need her.

But I also feel pain, the pain of knowing what my mother endured in her early years, and the thought of it haunts me to this day. And it is, frankly, hard for me to understand how God allowed the Holocaust to happen. I will never abandon my Judaism, but I have serious and unresolved questions.

I can remember when I was a child. World War II was over long before I was born, but I remember still fearing for my mother's welfare. In dreams I experienced frightening things happening to me. When I was eight or nine, I had a persistent nightmare. Earlier I used to love to go to the house of my parents' friend Roselee Borow. She had a huge fireplace, and at a very early age I used to sit mesmerized by the flickering flames it emitted. In my dream, however, a Frankensteinlike bogeyman called Hitler used to emerge from the flames and slit my eyelids with a razor. Until very recently, I couldn't tell my mother about it, although the dream is vivid in my mind to this day. When I finally told my mother of it, she wept. It was very difficult for me to tell her this, but perhaps it will help me to communicate more openly with my mother about these things that have haunted me since my early childhood.

I recall our trip to Hungary in 1972. I was only fifteen, but I could sense in my mother that she had once felt safe and familiar, yet in the end had found herself unprotected and vulnerable, and that she was reliving the terror and fright during our journey there. My one positive experience there was meeting and spending time with my uncle, my only other Hungarian relative who had survived. Even Israel failed to bring me tranquility. I don't want to be in places where life is in jeopardy.

I am not able to deal with the issues confronting the Second Generation. It is still too painful for me even to imagine what my mother went through. I avoid films and books about the Holocaust.

All this having been said, my mother is an anchor to me. She is, to risk repeating an overused phrase, my role model. Despite all she has suffered herself, she brings help and hope to others. She works steadily to better the world around her. She has provided and promoted for me the two most important values in my life: stability and security. I hope I can be for my daughter, Caryn, what my mother has been for me.

# Joseph Feldman

None of us can fully know the horrors my mother experienced, but at least we now have some awareness of these through all the books that have been published and all the facts that have been revealed about the Holocaust. We also know how our parents' sufferings in the Holocaust have affected the Second Generation.

One personal lesson I have learned is the importance of family. My mother lost virtually all of the family with whom she had grown up and shared the earliest years of her life. In one day nearly all of them disappeared, including my grandparents. I have learned from her experience to cherish my parents.

The Holocaust has taught me that one cannot know what will happen a year—or even a day—from now. So we must live every day to the fullest and take nothing for granted; above all, we must love and appreciate those closest to us while they are still here.

In high school I learned what it meant to be a member of a minority and to hear remarks about Jews. But I never flinched from expressing who I was, and I even got in trouble a few times when I fought back after being called names. In college I became friendly with a member of the Plainfield Country Club. By this time I was conspicuously wearing a Jewish star around my neck.

Once at the club I wore a shirt open at the neck, exposing the star. My friend advised me to conceal it while there. I responded by opening another button. Then I walked out, never to return.

But my feelings about being Jewish were positive as well as defensive. I belonged to Young Judea, went to Jewish camps during the summer, attended religious services, and maintained a proud Jewish identity.

One of my most vivid memories was of my trip to Hungary with my mother. I was not even bar mitzvah at that time. While visiting my paternal grandfather's synagogue, I ascended the *bimah* and began praying alongside the rabbi. I remember meeting my grandfather's brother Henrik, the only survivor of my mother's Hungarian family, and seeing the emotion and anguish in his eyes. I also remember my Israel trip with my mother in 1981, when I was twenty-one. At one point, I remember, people were struggling to get on one of the Israeli buses, and before me flashed an image of the suffocating struggle for breathing room in the railroad cars bound for Auschwitz.

I have had a great deal of trouble dealing with God. How could God have allowed what happened to happen to His children? I have never received a satisfactory answer, but the most unsatisfactory answer came from my teacher at Hebrew school, who responded by taking a pencil and breaking it in half, simply to indicate that God can do what God wishes. I will always be a proud Jew, but I will always have questions about God's role in the Holocaust.

As for my mother, as long as I have known her she has never lost her faith or her ability to care for others, whether the young or the elderly or the infirm, besides caring for her family. Her ability to talk plainly and eloquently about her experiences to all ages and all groups, including Germans, has never ceased to amaze me. I not only love her for what she does, but respect her commitment as well.

# Caryn Horowitz

Caring, understanding, thoughtful—these are just a few words that describe my grandmother. She has done so much for me, and there are no words to describe my thanks to her.

When I was studying World War II and the Holocaust in fifth grade, we were asked to write a poem to express the events that took place during the time. Most of the children wrote simple acrostics, but I started to write and came up with this:

I'm packing to leave Hungary and don't have any time.
It seems being a Jew has now become a crime.
The Nazis came to power and have made many rules.
I can't do simple things, like go to public schools.
Hitler came to power in 1933.
Everybody's running to try to capture me.
Hitler, now the Fuehrer, gives speeches on the radio.
The kids who were once my friends have now become
     my foes.
Now my trusty journal has become my only friend.
When will this Nazi-ruled world come to an end?

I read the poem to my grandmother, and she loved it. She made me feel good by complimenting me. That's the way she is. She'll always make people feel great, no matter what.

The more I think about it, the more I know I could not do without her. I love her and never want to leave her. I love you, Mama.

# APPENDIX

# E

## Uncle Sanyi and Aunt Erzike

I *recovered and translated from Hungarian the following letter, which my Uncle Sanyi had written to my Aunt Minnie Boehm and her family in New York. A note written at the bottom of that letter by his sister Erzike, or Elizabeth, follows Sanyi's letter. Uncle Sanyi's letter, dated March 31, 1941, reflects the creeping but still vaguely ominous sense that was engulfing the Jews of Hungary, particularly those living in rural areas with little access to what was happening in the rest of Europe, who were still unaware of the horror that awaited us. At the time my uncle wrote it, he was unemployed and in dire economic straits.*

My Dearest Sister,

We received your letter, which you wrote on February 5. It took almost two months for it to arrive. It brought us a lot of happiness.

I am making sure to write back to you today because I know how anxiously you are waiting for mail. I have to write now also because we don't know how long we will be allowed to write to you. We don't know from day to day what will happen in this upside-down world.

Henrik was just here, and we read your letter over and over together. He had to go home and did not have time to write now. He said he will write to you soon.

Our beloved mother carries your letter around, and she asks whoever is near to read and reread the letter to her. She can't see the small letters any more. Our nerves are not the most stable, and we don't have the most patience with her. The poor soul has no idea what is going on in the world, and we don't tell her anything that is bad.

She cries a lot for all of you and for us too.

Last year all three of us were in the work brigade. She had enough bitterness from that!

Everything around us is so confused! We have nothing good to look forward to, and we are ready for the worst. We are all so depressed that when the worst comes we will not be surprised. I know a lot of blood will be spilled before the sun will shine on us again and peace will come.

I know this much! My hope has almost run out, but we still retain some faith in God's help. And this alone keeps us going, even though we are suffering.

Hopefully, there will be an end to all the sadness. The time will come when we can hold our heads high; we will be with all our friends and family, and we will be able to look directly and accusingly into the eye of the evil that brought on all this madness.

We thank you for the beautiful invitation. We wish all love and happiness to our Klarika [Minnie's daughter, Clara, who had recently gotten married]. May God give happiness to all the days of their lives together. I hope that Ethel [Sanyi's sister] also attended the wedding and felt as much happiness and pride as you did.

You, Herminka, did everything that was humanly possible. You brought up your children correctly, the same way our parents brought us up. . . .

Please do not worry about us. . . . We are not suffering any deprivations. Until I can find some work, I will stay here with Elizabeth. I have some savings left. And I would rather pay her for room and board than give it to a stranger. . . .

I don't think we would be able to leave Hungary, even if everything turned out to be in our favor. At our ages, it hardly pays to go out and start a life in a new country. I don't think, at this point, our nerves could take it.

If the climate here becomes normal again, I promise I will come to you for a long visit.

I still hope that, with the help of our dear God, I can get some work. . . . Last week I went to Pest and learned that Aunt Kati is very sick. The government took away their business too, and I don't know how they will exist. . . .

Next week Joseph will come up, and then, when we will all be together, I will have a picture taken of all of us, and I will send it to you.

I am sorry that your husband has to work so hard; for some of us, no matter how hard we work, we cannot get ahead.

I think I did write enough for now, my dear ones. One does not know what to write because our life is so difficult here that we can't we can't even begin to write about it. But I know that I have to write because you are waiting for mail. Now I will leave some space to Erzike to write too. She did not have a chance to say anything in the last letter, and you did reprimand me for that. Now I'm making sure that she writes something.

My loved ones, may the good God give you all good things. With much love, I send you many kisses.

Your brother,
Sanyi

My Dearest Sister,

I will just write small, as the space is small. Sanyi told you everything. I haven't much patience to write. I wish your children much love and happiness, and to you also. Ethel, dear, to you I wish good health. May every wish of yours come true. We did receive the money, and we thank you. To all of you, I send love and kisses.

Erzike

# Uncle Henrik

The following letter, which I have translated from Hungarian, was written by my Uncle Henrik, the only other survivor of my family, a short time after his return to Sarospatak. It is dated December 1945. "Herminka" is my Aunt Minnie, and "Fredikem" is Fred, her husband.

Dearest Herminka, Fredikem, and Family,
On November 23, your letter arrived. Reading your letter makes me feel good. All other feelings are painful.

When I read your writing after so many years apart, it seems as though we were talking together.

But I cry with pain when I think of the past, and nothing relieves me. I even dream at night of my suffering.

I am trying to gain some strength in order to tell you of all that has happened to me since April 1944. On the 16th we were all collected—all the Jews—and we were locked in cattle cars and shipped off the Auschwitz, a place we had never heard of before. After the trip, which is indescribable, we arrived there, and we were immediately separated. All the old, the sick, the mothers and children were immediately killed in the gas chambers. That is how my wife, my children, my mother, father, and brothers-in-law were murdered.

I was lucky to remain together with our brothers, Sanyi and Joseph.

Joseph was soon taken from us. He couldn't withstand the hard work. He was shipped back to Auschwitz on a transport with others who were in no shape to do any kind of hard labor.

You can just imagine what happened to him.

I worked together with Sanyi until February. Then I got sick with a very high fever and was put in the camp hospital. By then the Russians were pretty close, and we were left with the thought that, at the last minute, the Germans would put a flame to the hospital and burn us all up.

However, they rushed to ship out the ones most ill from the hospital. This is how I was separated from Sanyi. . . . I made up my mind that, at any cost, I must try to stay alive.

Later I found out that they were just chasing the prisoners from place to place. From a transport of three thousand, perhaps three hundred stayed alive. Sanyi disappeared or died of hunger or they shot him. . . .

These are very difficult words to write, but it is even worse to live through it all.

Can one's brain even accept the way they killed all these men: with hunger, beatings, shootings, and worse?

With me was Erzike's husband, who, on February 14, died of pain or hunger. Another brother-in-law, Heinrich Gazo, died five days later.

I somehow survived. On May 9, my birthday, the Russians arrived and we were liberated.

With sores all over my feet, I started for home. I hoped that I would find someone at home. At that point, I didn't really know how many had actually survived and how many had died.

During the trip home I contracted typhoid and ended up in the hospital in the Czech Republic for three weeks. I was always burning up with fever; otherwise I would have gone home. I even tried to shake down the thermometer to show that I was fever free. I was not thinking correctly, and I left the hospital still feverish and started home. It took me ten days on train and by foot to get home, and I was sick the whole time.

What I was dreading all the way home was a reality: no one of our family had survived. Our home was emptied of everything. In four rooms I was unable to find a single piece of furniture. . . .

My fever was still present, and I could not eat because my stomach had shut down. . . . My position looked hopeless. I weighed 67 kilograms [148 pounds], and on my return I weighed 42 kilograms [93 pounds]. . . . I felt death lingering over me.

It looked as though that was what was written in my book of life.

But a few days later, a very good friend from Sarospatak also came home. She had lost both of her parents. . . . I must tell you, she brought some life back into me. I remained in bed with a high fever, and she was at my side. Without her, in my very weak condition, I would surely have died.

I felt very thankful to her. Day by day, we got closer. Just like me, she had no one else. . . . We knew we had only each other, so we made up our minds to belong to each other. We love each other. She is a wonderful person, giving and caring. Together, we will try to get over the nightmare we went through. . . .

I do understand, Herminka, that you must be shocked to read all this. I hope you understand my condition and my decision. Bozske feels that you are having problems accepting our marriage because you did not respond to our announcement. I have told her that we are a very loving sister and brother and that you will love her too.

She knew my whole family in Sarospatak; her name was Bozske Weinberger, and I can say only good things about her.

During the deportation, she was together with Elizabeth and Margit. They were separated while in camp.

She will write to you, and you will see from her writing what a wonderful person she is and love her as you love me.

We are working together in the Jewish National Agency in Sarospatak. I am the Executive Director. This organization helps Jews returning from the camps to find homes and to deal with other matters. Bozske is the Secretary of the Agency and she also keeps the books.

We are together all day, since our offices are near to each other. We have a bedroom, a bathroom, and a kitchen. This is more than enough for us, since we have no big needs. . . . We are happy that God has been with us in all our days.

I would love to come to you; I'd even go tomorrow; everyone wants to go either to America or Palestine.

There is nothing that ties us to this country any more. The hatred toward Jews is the same as it was before.

We have nothing here. And as soon as an opportunity arises, we would like to leave this place with your help. They have even taken the vineyards away from us, and until today I am unable to reclaim it. Your share they should never have taken away. I will write about it some more next time. I will explain what you have to do to reclaim it. . . . We are waiting for a letter in which you are inviting us to come to you in America. . . . I am asking you to look into this and to send papers as soon as you can. We have to apply at the consulate here for exit visas.

Bozske is a licensed beautician. She has already managed a salon in Budapest.

I am very happy that you are all well and are all together as a family. I hope to hold you all soon in my embrace.

Now we must stay in contact with each other. Let us not wait for each others' letters. Just keep writing and sending mail. . . . My happier days are when I can get mail from you. . . . With much love I embrace you and your whole family, each one of you individually.

Henrik